W9-BVT-776

THE NORMAN WILLIAMS PUBLIC LIBRARY
WOODSTOCK, VERMONT 05091

Cape May Primitive. Up to date version of an early nineteenth century rug. Hooked by Viola George. Shown in color on back cover.

746.7
MOSHIMER

The Complete Book of
Rug Hooking

by Joan Moshimer

DOVER PUBLICATIONS, INC., NEW YORK

ACKNOWLEDGMENTS

My sincere thanks to the many people without whose help this book would not have been possible: photographers Reg van Cuylenburg and Richard Cheek; Daniel Lohnes and William Blandford of the Society for the Preservation of New England Antiquities; Joel Kopp of America Hurrah Antiques; Bates Lowry of the University of Massachusetts, Boston; and the following rug hookers and teachers: Patience Agnew, Anita Allen, Betty Asquith, Anne Ashworth, Alice Beatty, the late Milda Berry, Bernice Bickum, Ethel Bruce, Pauline and William Burdick, Virginia Burgeson, Viola George, Ruth Gillette, Hallie Hall, Ruth Hall, Lydia Hicks, the late Ruth Higgins, Margaret Hooper, Louise Johnson, Mary Langzettel, Priscilla Lindley, Polly Merrill, Elizabeth Palmer, Marianna Sausaman, Abby Simms, Grassie Ward.

J. M.

Cushing's Perfection Dyes, color-coordinated fabric swatches and Craftsman Studio patterns for rug hooking are available from W. Cushing & Co., P.O. Box 351, Kennebunkport, Maine 04046.

Copyright © 1975, 1989 by Joan Moshimer.
All rights reserved under Pan American and International Copyright Conventions.

Published in Canada by General Publishing Company, Ltd., 30 Lesmill Road, Don Mills, Toronto, Ontario.
Published in the United Kingdom by Constable and Company, Ltd.

The Complete Book of Rug Hooking, published by Dover Publications, Inc., in 1989, is a corrected and slightly abridged republication of the third edition of *The Complete Rug Hooker: A Guide to the Craft,* published by Leith Publications, Kennebunkport, Maine in 1986, and originally published by the New York Graphic Society in 1975. All the photographs originally printed in color are reproduced here in black-and-white. In addition, twenty-one are also shown in color in an eight-page color section and on the covers. The List of Suppliers has been omitted from this edition.

Manufactured in the United States of America
Dover Publications, Inc., 31 East 2nd Street, Mineola, N.Y. 11501

Library of Congress Cataloging-in-Publication Data

Moshimer, Joan.
  [Complete rug hooker]
  The complete book of rug hooking / by Joan Moshimer.
      p.   cm.
  Reprint. Originally published: The complete rug hooker. Boston : New York Graphic Society, 1975.
  ISBN 0-486-25945-5
  1. Rugs, Hooked. I. Title.
  [TT850.M67 1989]
  746.7′4—dc19
                            88-32119
                                CIP

Contents

Vendome. Designed by the author, hooked by Betty Asquith. Motifs from oriental rugs can be easily adapted for the square mesh of burlap; in fact, they were a frequent source of motifs for the earliest rug hookers. For this rug, the entire design of an oriental rug is simulated. A large variety of wools was used to duplicate the oriental's intricate coloring. Shown in color on inside back cover.

Coral roses and circles—an old rug from "Beauport," Gloucester, Massachusetts has retained its cheerful colors. Here a few flowers and simple shaded circles combine to make a dramatic pattern. (Courtesy Society for the Preservation of New England Antiquities)
Shown in color on front cover.

Canadian. Maker unknown. In this early Aubusson-inspired rug, the roses and scrolls have been sculpted with shears, a distinguishing feature of early Canadian rugs. Reds predominate with rich browns and greens against a mellow tan background. The somewhat crudely drawn scrolls are redeemed by artistic coloring. (Private collection)

1 The American Tradition of Rug Hooking

Rug hooking reached a creative peak in early nineteenth-century America (in both New England and the Canadian Maritime Provinces), although both skilled and unskilled hookers were handicapped by a basic lack of materials and had to rely on their own ingenuity. Before the widespread availability of burlap (after 1850), feed sacks—after they were washed, stretched, and pieced—were frequently used as the foundation material. The fabric to be hooked into the foundation came primarily from clothing no longer usable; the otherwise-worthless woven materials were washed, sorted, and then colored in homemade dyes extracted from local plants (yellows were obtained from golden rod, marsh marigold, sumac, oak, and sunflower; greens from mint, ash, and smartweed; reds from cranberry, sumac, bloodroot, dogwood, alder, and elm; blues from grape, sycamore, and larkspur; browns from walnut, butternut, and alder). The dyed materials were then cut into narrow strips to be worked into the

1

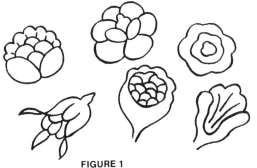

FIGURE 1

foundation using hooks fashioned from nails, bone-handled forks, or whatever else was readily available.

For some, creating a design was most likely a difficult task, although husbands and children undoubtedly took a keen interest in the planning of the current "mat" design, contributing ideas and suggestions. Others adapted bits of embroidery or a treasured piece of decorated china. Most early rug hookers, though, relied on their surroundings for inspiration. Houses, barnyard scenes, a cat frolicking with her kittens, dogs, horses, hens, roosters, a horseshoe for good luck, and the always beloved flowers from the summer garden—these, recreated in simple form on the burlap, became abstractions of the real blossoms, beautiful in their own way.

No fancy methods of transferring the designs for the early rug hooker—she took a piece of charcoal and drew directly onto an old feedsack or other foundation material. This free-wheeling method accounts for the simplicity and naive charm which characterizes so many of the old rugs. Many a strange-looking animal was the result of a freehand attempt to portray some barnyard creature or favorite pet. Often, most unlikely objects were combined in these primitive designs—such as horses, birds, trees, stars, and crescent moon—with no attempt to show proper size relationship or perspective. But as amusing as these early designs are, they all clearly reveal the personality of the creator; they were truly a means of self-expression for the maker and as such have great charm and individuality.

Rug hooking was a craft confined not only to women. Sailors frequently hooked rugs on their long sea journeys; they used canvas as the foundation material and short strands of yarn or rope. Full-rigged ships, anchors, and whaling scenes were favorite designs. It is easy to imagine the sailor's wives or sweethearts, inspired by these efforts, taking to the craft with enthusiasm.

Geometric patterns have always been popular with rug hookers—primarily because they are simple to design. Early rug hookers used the burlap mesh as guidelines, drawing directly on the burlap with charcoal or using everyday objects as templates. The kitchen plate, for example, was a

Checks and arrows in a mostly geometric antique rug from "Beauport," Gloucester, Massachusetts. The basic motifs, in panels, are subtly varied and combined with scrolls. The colors have faded to appealing soft tones, but the vibrant hues of the back of the rug remind us that many early rugs were originally very colorful.
(Courtesy Society for the Preservation of New England Antiquities)
Illustrated on color plate A.

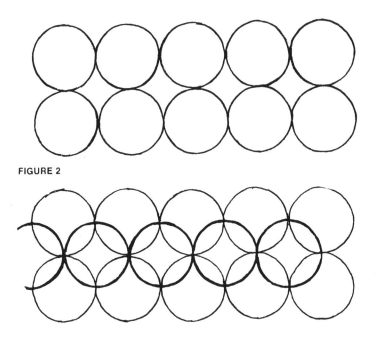

FIGURE 2

popular designing aid; it was drawn around as many times as necessary for an overall design (the circles side by side or overlapping) or it was used as a stencil to provide interesting borders. The antique rug on page vii, from "Beauport," in Gloucester, Massachusetts, is a stunning example of how

FIGURE 3

effective a simple circular design can be. Geometric designs were not only comparatively simple to design, but could also be very attractively hooked with what rug hookers call "hit-or-miss": multicolored leftover materials hooked in

Simple paisleys combined with conventional flowers   **FIGURE 4**

An elaborate paisley as seen in paisley shawls

FIGURE 5

5

Opposite page: The Fireman. Made in New England in the early twentieth century, this rug carries on the grand tradition of the amusing—or uplifting—verse worked into the design. The tradition might well be revived by hookers today. (Courtesy America Hurrah Antiques, New York)

Right: A kitchen plate or bowl probably made the template for this gay design of variously colored circles arranged at apparent random on a dark background. The design technique is still a good one and can be adapted for modern geometrics. Rug from "Beauport," Gloucester, Massachusetts. (Courtesy Society for the Preservation of New England Antiquities) Illustrated on color plate E.

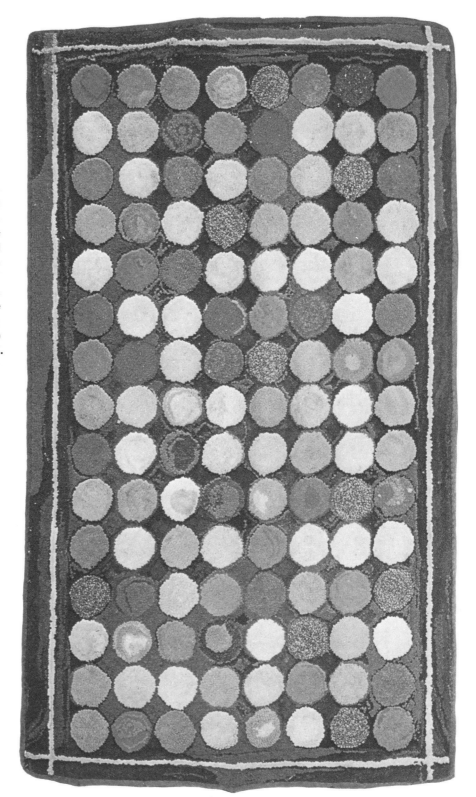

House with Rainbow. Hooked by Lucy Barnard, 1850-1875. The maker of this wonderful hooked rug was not perturbed by rules of perspective; the flowers and trees dwarf the house—reputedly the home of a friend of Lucy Barnard's in Dixfield, Maine—and reach right up to the rainbow. The rainbow, symbolic in Christian theology of pardon and reconciliation, was a popular subject with early rug hookers—undoubtedly because of the lovely colors as well as the symbolism—but existing examples of it are rare.
(Courtesy Metropolitan Museum of Art, Sansbury-Mills Fund, 1961)

without further dyeing. Frequently, the different colors and assorted textures of leftover wools created a fascinating effect despite an otherwise dull, uninspired design.

Oriental rugs, found only in the homes of the wealthy in early America, provided inspiration for many hooked rugs in more modest homes. The intricate motifs of oriental rugs were enlarged and simplified for the loosely woven burlap of hooked rugs. The paisley pattern, for example—a motif well-known from paisley shawls (named for the town in Scotland where they were woven) as well as from oriental rugs from which the motif was originally adapted—was used frequently in repeat designs or combined with floral motifs in early hooked rugs. As with geometric patterns, the paisley could also be effectively hooked with hit-or-miss materials.

During the middle 1800s, Edward Sands Frost, an enterprising man from Biddeford, Maine, contributed to the development of the craft into a home industry by creating stencils of tin and then selling them from his peddler's wagon to the grateful housewives along his route. During his travels

8

around the New England countryside, while visiting in the homes of his customers, he had seen firsthand the sometimes crude and unsuccessful attempts that were made to design attractive rugs. His own wife was working on a rug, using a poorly made hook. To quote Frost in the Biddeford *Times* in 1888:

> I noticed she was using a very poor hook, so, being a machinist, I went to work and made the crooked hook. . . . I got interested in the rug. I "caught the fever" as they used to say. So every evening I worked on the rug. After four evenings . . . I told my wife I thought I could make a better design. . . . So after we finished our rug I got a piece of burlap . . . I wrote my first design on paper and then put it on the cloth. . . . I got orders for twenty or more patterns like it within three days. So you see I got myself into business right away. There was not money enough in it to devote my whole time to the business, and as the orders came in faster than I could fill them I began, Yankee-like, to study some way to do them quicker. Then the idea of stencilling presented itself to me. . . . I went out into my stable where I had some old iron and some old wash boilers I had bought for their copper bottoms, took the old tin off of them and made my first stencil out of it. I began making small stencils of single flowers, scrolls, leaves, buds, etc. each one on a small plate; then I could with a stencil brush print in ink in plain figures much faster than I could sketch. Thus I reduced ten hours labor to two and a half hours. I then had the art down fine enough to allow me to fill my orders, so I began to print patterns and put them in my peddler's cart and offer them for sale. The news of my invention of stamped rugs spread like magic . . . I at once became known as Frost, the rug man. . . .

Frost's business became a great success, but it had the unfortunate effect of stifling the creative efforts of many. It is the earlier rugs, usually inspired by daily surroundings and frequently intense expressions of personality, that we cherish especially; but the gifted could take a printed pattern and by an unusual choice of color, use of textures, or interesting deviation from the stenciled lines, create a personal work. The lion rug on page 45 is an example of an unusually free-wheeling adaptation.

Frost sold his business in 1876. The metal stencils, nearly four tons of them, were eventually sold to Charlotte K. Stratton, who used them in her pattern business for a number of years before selling them to the Henry Ford Museum in Dearborn, Michigan. Today the museum prints the old designs from the stencils, and sells them through their handsome catalog. Each summer Greenfield Village and the Henry Ford Museum hold a hooking bee and exhibition stressing the type of hooking similar to that done during the nineteenth century, in an effort to preserve the old methods.*

About the same time that Edward Sands Frost was beginning his pattern business, another veteran of the Civil War worked as a dyer in a small woolen mill in the northern Maine town of Foxcroft. Local housewives, some of them rug hookers, begged him for dyes for use in their own homes. Wainwright Cushing sensed that the time was right for a complete line of chemical "mill-type" dyes to replace the time-consuming task of vegetable dyeing, and in his spare time at home began to develop such a line. His first colors were turkey red and black, but he eventually developed the complete spectrum, selling them by mail. The Cushing Company, now owned by Craftsman Studio, Kennebunkport, Maine 04046, thriving to this day, still counts rug hookers among its most enthusiastic customers.

By the end of the nineteenth century, with the growing demand for low-priced machine-made carpeting, the popularity of hooked rugs declined. The once-prized rugs which had graced the front parlor were often relegated to the kitchen and from there to the woodpile. Or they were rolled up and tucked away into the far corners of dusty attics and barns. For decades, hooked rugs were sadly neglected and ill-appreciated—except for a few far-sighted individuals who recognized hooked rugs as a valuable part of our past to be preserved. Ralph Burnham was one such man. Hooked rugs were brought to his business in Ipswich, Massachusetts, to be cleaned and repaired. In one of Burnham's advertising booklets, he stated that in 1928 more than 5,000 rugs were repaired by his "corps of experts" (his words).

Wanting to preserve the old designs, Burnham copied the

*Since the original publication of this book, the museum has discontinued the hooking exhibition and the sale of the Frost patterns. The designs, adapted to today's printing methods, are now available from W. Cushing & Co.

Classic floral in contemporary colors. This antique rug from "Beauport," Gloucester, Massachusetts, is unusual for its vivid chartreuse and yellow tones. (Collection Society for the Preservation of New England Antiquities)

rug designs as they passed through his hands and thus began a superb collection. He began to print the old patterns on burlap and made them available for sale. In one of his 1937 advertisements, he said, "These are, for the most part, taken from famous rugs of the past. Over the years we have collected examples of American hooked rugs. When we found one which showed great merit in design our artists made faithful copies thereof and from these we have distributed them throughout the country as a part of the heritage of the past."

It has only been recently that rug hooking has received the long-overdue recognition from museums, galleries, and the public it deserves as a rich part of our heritage. But more important, not only is appreciation growing for hooked rugs

11

Woman in a Garden. The maker of this charming old rug simplified a visually complicated subject, using bold, flat forms effectively.
(Collection Burton and Helaine Fendelman)

Opposite page, top: Welcome Home. Origin unknown, 1800-1875. "Welcome" rugs—such as this charming, well-balanced design—never lose their appeal, probably because they express so clearly the warmth associated with home.
(Courtesy The Henry Francis du Pont Winterthur Museum)

Opposite page, bottom: Origin unknown. A very effective antique rug in which just one motif is used. The leaves are separated from one another by the light, bright shades used on the edges where the upper leaves are set against darker ones underneath. The background, hooked in straight lines, provides an interesting contrast to the varied directional lines of the leaves.
(Private collection)

Waldoboro, Maine, 1820-1850. Maker unknown. This early primitive design of gaily drawn flowers, leaves, and birds, was hooked with multicolored leftover cotton strips. The cotton was used "as is"—that is, without further dyeing—and at one time, the rug may have been very bright, but today the colors have faded pleasantly to gentler hues.
(Courtesy The Henry Francis du Pont Winterthur Museum)

made in the folk-art tradition, but the craft itself is being enthusiastically revived as a means of self-expression. That is what this book is all about.

14

2 Fundamentals of Rug Hooking

Many people have long seen and admired hooked rugs without having the least idea how they are made. Traditional hooking is the process of pulling up (in loops about ⅛″-¼″ high) narrow strips of wool fabric through the mesh of a foundation material. The loops, pulled up many times close together, form a pile. A hook (like a crochet hook set into a wooden handle) is used to pull up the loops—hence the term "hooking."

Burlap is commonly used for the foundation, although monk's cloth and certain other materials are used to a lesser

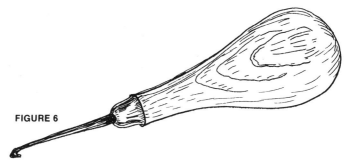

FIGURE 6

15

extent. For the purpose of this book, the foundation will be called burlap. Today's burlap does not bear much similarity to the old loosely woven hessian feed bags of our great-grandmothers' day. It is more correctly called "jute cloth" by the manufacturers in Scotland, since they no longer use the coarse outer layers of the plant, but instead use the stronger, fine inner fibers.

Almost all weights of wool can be used in hooking. The heavier the wool, the narrower it should be cut; conversely, the lighter-weight wools should be cut wider. The ideal weight is closely woven 100% wool flannel, which is soft and pliable.

Loosely woven wools and tweeds are hard to hook because they tend to pull apart when cut into strips. You can sometimes shrink them enough to make them usable, and it's well worth the effort because they are lovely when hooked in, lending their subtle colors and textures to your hooking. To shrink loosely woven materials, break all the usual rules for washing wools. Wash them in hot water and detergent, in the washing machine preferably, rinsing them in hot water and then cold.

Wool jersey and knitted material are not good to use, except possibly here and there in small amounts, because they tend to mat down and lack the natural "springiness" of regular wool weaves. (Exception: jerseys work well in wall hangings. In fact, since durability is not a factor when choosing materials for a wall hanging, use any fiber you like: yarns, cut strips of fur, velvets, cottons, silk, etc.)

Today, wool often has a percentage of some of the man-made fibers—this is all right as long as the percentage is small. You may notice when you dye this wool that the man-made fiber may not take the dye as well. This will give some textural interest to your rug and is not objectionable. It is a little more difficult to cut than 100% wool.

Above all, remember this is a handcraft. Different weights and thicknesses can, and should, be used in the same rug. If you are insistent on using exactly the same weight and texture throughout your rug, then you'll produce a uniform, almost machine-made look which is certainly not the purpose of a handcraft. The most appealing hooked rugs result from wool strips of different colors and textures being worked into designs.

How to Cut the Wool

The wool, to hold together and not pull apart, must be cut on the straight of the material. If you look closely at your wool strip, it will look something like the sketch (fig. 7). The long fibers are what hold the material together; if it is cut even slightly on the bias, it will pull apart as you try to hook it. So be careful about the cutting.

The first step is to tear the wool into narrow strips about 3 or 4 inches wide. The length is a matter of choice. I suggest you make them about 12 inches long. The torn edge should be absolutely straight and will then make a perfect guide for cutting. A cutting machine is highly recommended. Although it is not essential to own one, it is a big saving in time and effort. They come with various interchangeable blades for cutting different widths from less than ⅛″ up to ¼″.

Again, let me emphasize, whether cutting by hand or machine, keep the strips on the straight of the material. The tweeds mentioned earlier generally are difficult to tear, but you can carefully cut them with your scissors using an easily seen thread as a guide, then cut them with your cutting machine to the desired width.

Frames

The purpose of a frame is to hold your burlap firmly taut. Many kinds are available, varying greatly in price. All are good and each variety has enthusiastic boosters. My personal choice is the oval hoop (18″ × 27″) which can be removed from its base and used with or without a stand. For the beginner, round 14″ hoops are available very reasonably, and even an old picture frame on which to thumbtack the burlap can be successfully used. The important thing is to get started—better and more efficient equipment can be acquired as time and money permit.

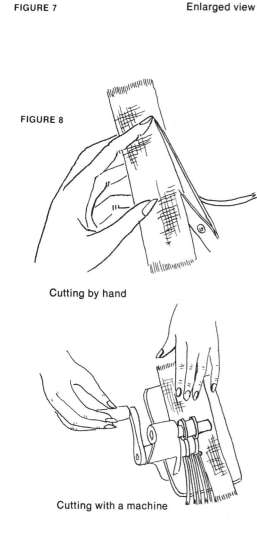

FIGURE 7   Enlarged view

FIGURE 8

Cutting by hand

Cutting with a machine

3 Basic Hooking Directions

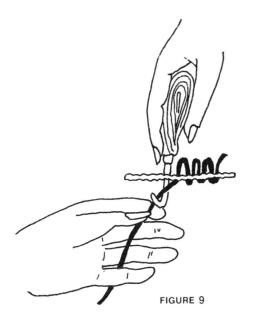

FIGURE 9

Traditional hooking is a craft that allows great freedom and flexibility. There is no one right way to hook; hooking is like handwriting in that all rug hookers develop their own individual style. The loops of wool are pulled up through the burlap to a height that looks and feels right to you. Some people tend to hook high and some low. The average height of the loops is about ⅛". You will find that the wider the strip of wool is cut, the higher the loop will be; for some primitive-type rugs, if the strips are cut by hand ¼" wide or wider, the pile may be ½" high (these rugs naturally require more wool). And of course, when the wool strips are cut wide, you will be skipping more meshes so that the loops are not too packed.

The hook is held in the right hand, above the pattern, and the strip of wool, which can be any desired length, usually about 12 inches long, is held in the left hand, underneath the pattern. (If you are left-handed, these positions are reversed.)

Push the hook through the burlap and slide the smooth

18

side of the shank down between your forefinger and thumb (the tip of the hook will touch the thumb) and let the tip catch hold of the wool strip (which is between the other thumb and forefinger). See Figure 9. Pull the end up to the top side to a height of about 1 inch. (All ends are pulled through to the top side, not left hanging underneath, and later cut off even with the top of the other loops. They become invisible in the pile.)

Now put the hook through the next hole and pull up a loop to a height of about ⅛″. Working from right to left, keep pulling up loops as evenly as you can, occasionally skipping a hole in the burlap to keep the loops from being packed too tightly. When the end of the strip is reached, be sure to bring it through to the top side and trim. If the wool is cut very fine (less than ⅛″), hook into almost every mesh. When using wider strips, skip as many holes as is necessary to have the loops comfortably touch each other. If you try to pack too many loops into the burlap you may strain it—yet if you have the loops too far apart the rug will not wear well. The surface should be firm but not packed.

At first, you may find that you are pulling out your previous loop as you hook, but don't be discouraged. This can be remedied by slightly twisting the hook *away* from you as you pull up. With practice you will find that you do this automatically.

Another tip: To avoid catching the burlap in the hook as you pull up, press the smooth side of the hook's shank against the burlap, thus making the hole bigger.

Practice hooking straight lines and curvy lines, then make little circles and fill them in. The underside should feel smooth to your fingertips with no loops, bumps, or tails left hanging. The top surface should be even, though any slight irregularities in the height of the loops will even out after the rug is in use on the floor. Beginners can be forgiven if they snip off the top of an occasional too-high loop. Make sure there are no open spaces; if you find any, fill them in promptly.

Don't be afraid to make a mistake—if you do, the offending loops can simply be pulled out and replaced.

You will accomplish more—and enjoy the craft more—if you can find a spot in your home where you can leave your frame and chair set up permanently. A "goose-neck" lamp, commonly used on power tools, attached to your rug frame, is a boon and gives you excellent light. With your frame always set up, you can sit down whenever you have a few minutes. Or whenever the cares of the day tend to crowd your mind, there, waiting for you, is your escape. If it is in the same room where you watch television, so much the better. The two occupations are compatible and some objectionable commercials are not so irritating if you don't have to look at them.

HEMMING AND BINDING

Before you begin hooking, machine stitch the burlap about 1″ beyond the outside line of your pattern, going across the corners as shown in Figure 10. Use the zigzag stitch or two rows of regular stitching. This is done to prevent fraying later when the rug is all finished and the excess burlap is removed. *(Do not cut off excess burlap at this time.)*

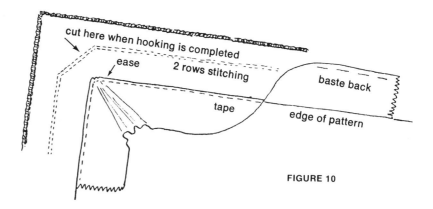

cut here when hooking is completed

ease

2 rows stitching

baste back

tape

edge of pattern

FIGURE 10

All rugs must be bound or faced on the edges because the greatest point of wear on a rug is its edge. A little extra care in this area will pay off in future years.

There are two ways to bind the edges of your rugs—one method is done before you begin hooking; the other, when you are finished—either method is good.

The tape used for binding is 1¼″-wide twilled tape. Plan to have it match or harmonize with the color of the edge of the rug. Do not use iron-on tape. If you are in doubt as to the exact color you will have on the edge, then use Method #2.

Method #1. To be done before you begin hooking. In this method, the tape should match or harmonize with the background color. Lay the tape on the pattern as shown and machine stitch ⅛″ in on the tape. Either ease it around corners or cut it off at each corner allowing 1″ extra. Then baste it back out of the way. Hook right up against the tape as close as possible and hook at least two rows parallel to it.

When the hooking is completed, the excess burlap is cut just beyond the two rows of machine stitching; both burlap and tape are folded back on an imaginary line ¼″ beyond the last row of hooking and mitered neatly at the corners. Hem by hand using heavy-duty thread. This will leave a quarter-inch "edge" beyond the hooking which is very attractive and practical. (Method #1 is shown in Figure 11.)

Method #2. To be done when you finish hooking. Hook the background right up to the line on pattern edge, putting at least two rows of hooking parallel to that line.

To match the tape color to the color of the rug, dye it (using white or a light color tape) when you dye your background wool. It won't match exactly but will blend nicely. Be sure to allow 4″ extra per yard for shrinkage.

When you have completed hooking, sew the tape by hand as close to the hooking as possible, using matching heavy-duty thread. Then cut off excess burlap and fold back and hem as in Method #1.

NOTE: The burlap and tape can be folded back all the way so that the tape is hidden from sight if you wish, but I recommend letting ¼″ of it show both for looks and wearability.

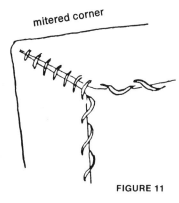

mitered corner

FIGURE 11

In finishing a circular or oval rug, it is easier to make your own tape by cutting strong cotton on the bias, or even using the same wool as was used in hooking the background and cutting it on the bias. Regular twill tape can be used but when it is turned back it is more difficult to hem because little "pleats" will form.

After you have completed hooking and binding your rug, place an old sheet on top of a rug already on the floor and put your finished hooked rug *face down* on it (I am assuming your rug is too large for the ironing board). Steam press thoroughly. It may be pressed again lightly on the top side if necessary.

PILLOWS

There are several ways to make a pillow. The two following methods are particularly easy.

Method #1. You may be lucky enough to find a readymade pillow that is the right size and color; then all you have to do is:
1. After hooking is completed and the piece is steam-pressed, sew two rows of machine stitching (⅛″ apart) about ¾″ beyond the last row of hooking; then cut off burlap just beyond the stitching.
2. Carefully turn all excess burlap to back and steam press it down thoroughly.
3. Center on purchased pillow and blind stitch it in place.

Method #2. To make a simple round pillow you will need: piece of wool, corduroy, or velveteen in a harmonizing color for back, which is the same diameter as hooked piece plus 1½″. Enough decorative cord to go around hooked piece. Muslin-covered pillow form which is slightly larger in diameter than hooked piece.
1. Follow step one in Method #1.

2. Cut backing material the same size as hooked piece (including the extra ¾″ beyond hooking).

3. Place hooked piece and backing together, right sides inside, then baste three-quarters of the way around.

4. Using a zipper foot, machine stitch together, burlap side up, as close to the last row of hooking as possible, three-quarters of the way around.

5. Carefully hand hem excess burlap back onto hooking.

6. Turn inside out, insert pillow and (turning under excess ¾″ of backing) blind stitch front and back in place.

7. Blind stitch decorative cord in place at edge.

MAKING FRINGE

Not all rugs have fringe on them, but some rugs, such as orientals and contemporary ones, look much better *with* fringe. (See Beverly Meadow, page 128.) It is, of course, a matter of choice.

You can tie in the fringe color to a main color in the rug if you wish, or just leave it its own natural color, which will change in time to a mellow tan.

There are several yarns to choose from. Paternayan has one that is strong and moth-proof. A strong, natural, "fisherman-sweater"-type yarn is good too, and takes the dye well if you choose to dye it.

The following directions, given to me by a good friend, Ruth Hall, a retired rug designer and teacher, call for whipped edges (along the long sides if the rug is rectangular), with the fringe on the ends.

Do *not* put binding on the rug until after the fringe is on. Before beginning the hooking, put two rows of machine stitching close together about 1″ outside the outer edge of pattern. (This will prevent fraying later on when it is time to cut off the excess burlap.)

When hooking is completed, do *not* cut off the excess burlap, but turn it under on the two long sides, leaving about ⅛″ of burlap showing.

With darning needle and rug yarn, whip over and over to cover the ⅛″ exposed fold of burlap. On the narrow ends of the rug where fringe is to go, turn the burlap under, leaving just slightly more than ⅛″ showing. Using your rug hook (or a crochet hook), make a row of single crochet across (or alternately, with the darning needle, make a row of blanket stitch across).

Go back to the beginning and make a second row of single crochet all the way across. Next, cut a quantity of 5″ lengths of yarn (for 2½″ fringe). An easy way to do this is to wind the yarn over and over a 2½″-wide strip of cardboard, then to cut the yarn carefully. Then take one piece, fold it in half, and hold it between thumb and forefinger of left hand (see fig. 12). Put hook through first single crochet (or blanket stitch) and pull loop through about ½″, then knot by putting ends of yarn through the loop and pulling them taut (see fig. 13).

Repeat in every single crochet all the way across. Next, cut off excess burlap *beyond* the two rows of machine stitching. This is covered by rug tape, stitched on by hand.

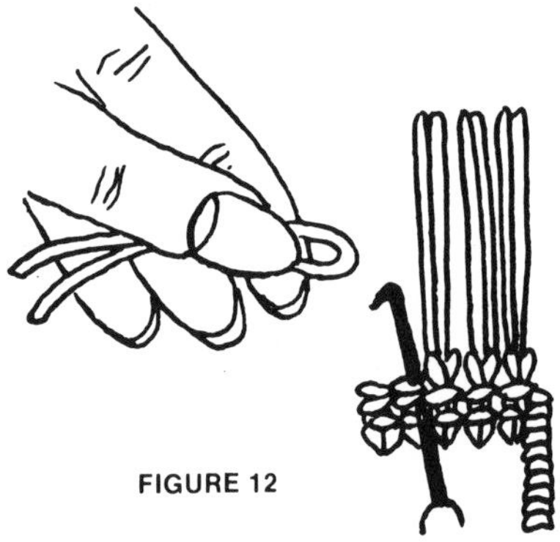

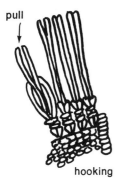

FIGURE 12

pull

hooking

FIGURE 13

See page 3.

Plate A

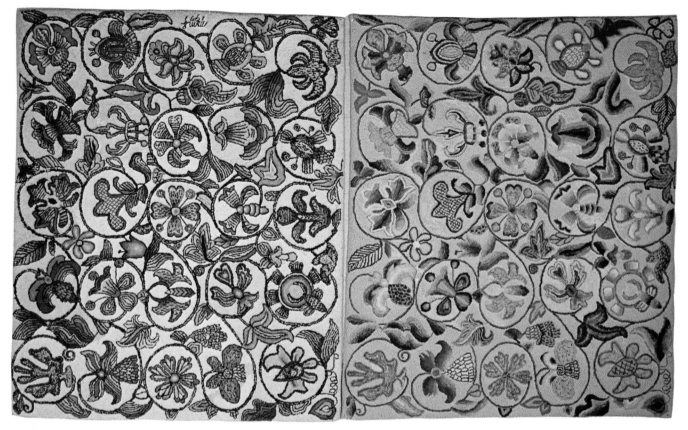

See page 48.

See page 132.

Plate B

See page 132.

See page 132.

Plate C

See page 44.

See page 44.

Plate D

See page 7.

Plate E

See page 53.

See page 56.

Plate F

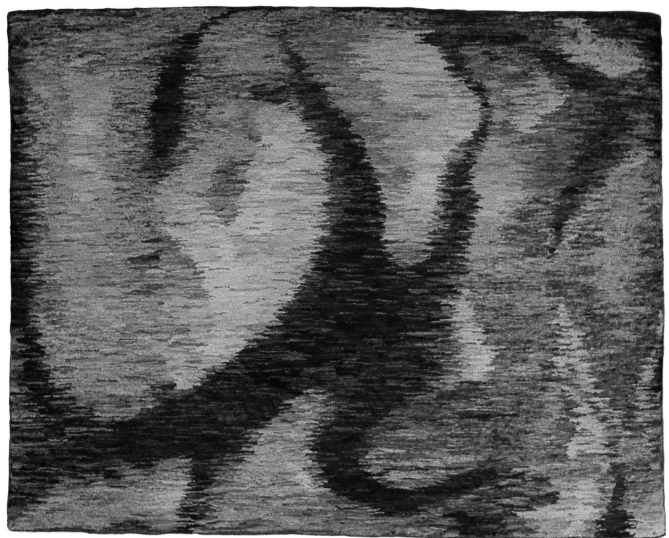

See page 136.

See page 128.

See page 128.

Plate G

See page 52.

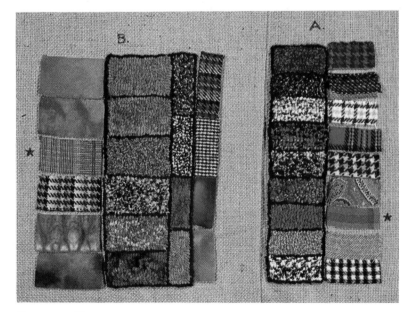

See page 48.

See page 52.

Plate H

4 Backgrounds

The background of a rug, *always* hooked after the design is completed, is usually the largest area; therefore the choice of color is an important decision. When hooking the design of a rug, the background color must always be kept in mind, checking often to make sure that the design will show up well against it. Whether you choose to hook a dark or light background will depend largely on individual preferences. Medium tones, because they are tricky to work with, should be avoided until you are more experienced. Generally speaking, keep your background in either soft, grayed light tones or dark, rich values. By doing this you will quickly see how well the designs look against them.

Where the rug is to go in your home is an important consideration. For instance, if it is to go in a dark hall or a corner which does not receive much daylight, then a wise choice might be a light background, such as soft green, beige, cream, pale gray, or soft pale gold. If the area where it is to go receives a lot of light, then the choice may be one of the darker tones, including black (preferably antique black), dark blue, navy, wine, deep green, rich brown, or eggplant.

Whatever you choose, remember that it is a *back*ground, and it must not be so bright that it overshadows the design in importance. It should stay in the *back*ground, setting off the design to good advantage. Exception: in a very modern rug you may decide on a bright and vivid background.

ANTIQUE BLACK

Antique black (see Chapter 9 for dyeing directions) is an excellent background color. Antique black—as opposed to the intense black we normally think of—is an unevenly dyed, rather blotchy black. It is a highly functional background color since dust, soil marks, and spots don't show up as they do against any extremely dark color.

When dyeing for backgrounds, either light or dark, I usually advise my pupils either to dye over a variety of wool textures or to crowd the wool into the dye pot so that it dyes slightly unevenly; then when the wool is hooked, there is that delightful fluctuation that is not only pleasing to the eye but is so practical.

HOOKING BACKGROUNDS

First, be sure to put one line of background color around the hooked design in order to "hold" the shapes. This applies *always,* no matter what method you use to hook the background. Backgrounds can be hooked in straight lines if you wish, but if you decide to do it that way, don't change your mind when part way through and go in other directions.

My personal choice for most rugs is the "random" method. After putting in the one line around the design, hook a wavy, meandering line any way you fancy. Then proceed to hook next to the line and to fill in spaces.

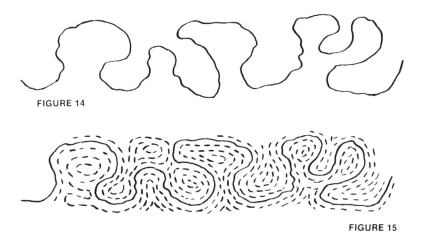

FIGURE 14

FIGURE 15

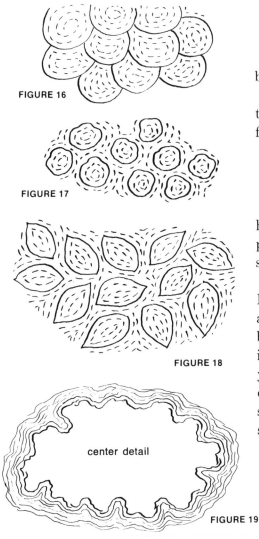

FIGURE 16

FIGURE 17

FIGURE 18

center detail

FIGURE 19

Remember, the design should *always* be hooked first, before the background is put in.

There are other ways to fill in backgrounds. Try some of them for yourself and you will soon discover your own favorites.

Outline the "scallops" first, then fill in.

Hook little circles first, then fill in and around them.

Hook the "leaves" first, then fill in and around them.

Your backgrounds will be more interesting to look at if hooked in one of these ways. An important advantage is their practicality—a rug hooked in one of these ways is slow to show soil marks.

While discussing the subject with my friend Ruth Hall of Rye, New Hampshire, she reminded me of an old tried-and-true method of hooking backgrounds which is excellent because if you should run out of your background wool, then it is easy to blend in a *similar* wool with it. Start hooking your background under the center detail. Then, following the contour, hook in a generally circular fashion. This way, should you run out, the new wool you use (probably being slightly different in value and color) will blend in evenly.

27

5 How to Transfer Designs

It is an easy process to enlarge and transfer one of the designs in this book to burlap. Art supply stores stock good-quality 100%-rag tracing vellum with ¼-inch grids printed on the paper. This kind of tracing paper will make your task much easier, and it is well worth searching for. It is an excellent aid in enlarging designs, and also good for use with the iron-on pattern pencil.

Of course, you can draw your own grid lines ¼ inch apart, horizontally and vertically, on plain tracing paper after you have traced your selected design and made any desired changes.

Either way, after your design is drawn on grid-marked tracing paper, decide how large you want your finished design to be, making a rectangle (or square) which has the overall dimensions of the size you want. Now divide your rectangle into the same number of squares or grids you used in your small design. Redraw over those lines with an indelible pen.

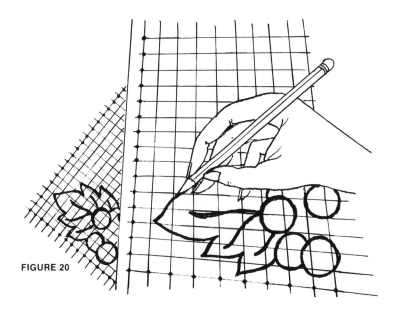

FIGURE 20

Using these squares as your guides, draw in the same design, square by square, that is in the smaller design. (Don't be afraid—it's easier than it sounds.)

This same method—in reverse—can be used to reduce a design. Remember, however, that it is much easier to draw your design *small* and then enlarge it. On a small sketch the proportions and balance show up more readily.

Transferring with dressmaker's carbon paper, usually successful for smooth fabrics, is difficult to do on the rougher surface of burlap. For this reason, the iron-on pattern pencil which makes an indelible blue line, is recommended. Using good-quality tracing paper, trace the design with an ordinary pencil, then turn the paper over and go over the lines with the pattern pencil, making strong (not faint) lines. Set iron for cotton and allow it to heat up well. Place design, pattern-pencil side down, on the burlap. Holding paper securely so that it doesn't move, run iron slowly over design. Be patient to allow enough time for the line to be transferred. (It turns blue as it transfers.) Lift a corner of the paper (carefully so that it doesn't move) to check. When all the lines are clearly showing on the burlap, it is ready. With care you can sometimes get two impressions from one tracing, but

29

Delft Daisies. Designed and hooked by
Joan Moshimer. A hand-painted Delft
dish inspired this simple design. It was
hooked in traditional blues, although any
color could have been used effectively.
Before the background was begun, three
lines were hooked around the outer edge
to preserve the shape of the piece. Then
the background was hooked with
random curving lines. Working this area
unevenly, instead of in straight
horizontal lines, gives the finished piece
a much more interesting appearance.

The Lute Player. Designed by Joan Moshimer, hooked by Ruth Gillette. An
ancient glazed earthenware bowl from Iran (opposite page, bottom) inspired
this rug, demonstrating that even the most unusual, unexpected designs
can be adapted for hooked rug patterns. Rich turquoises, blues, and golds
were used here; the background was hooked in various shades of turquoise
to achieve a marbleized appearance. Spot-dyed wools were used for the
clothing of the lute player and students.
(Minai bowl, Saljuq period, 12th-13th century. Courtesy The Metropolitan
Museum of Art. Gift of Mr. and Mrs. A. Wallace Chauncey)

31

Chinese Moth window valance. Designed by Joan Moshimer, hooked by Polly Merrill. This pattern of Chinese motifs was adapted from a blue and white Spode platter. By repeating and rearranging the motifs, the pattern can be made any size and shape desired.

after that it has to be discarded and a new tracing made if more are needed.

Another much overlooked but easy way to get a design onto burlap is to draw it *directly* on. Using a sharp-pointed pencil, it is easy to draw a straight line between two threads of the burlap. This is especially practical when drawing a geometric design as described in Chapter 14.

Or, if you have a color slide of a favorite pet or a scene that you would like to duplicate with your hook, put your burlap on the wall in place of the screen, then project the image of your slide on to it. Then it is an easy matter to draw the outlines of your design with a waterproof felt-tip pen on the burlap.

6 Primitive Rugs

Primitive rugs—rugs made in the folk-art tradition—are a rich source of design for today's rug hooker. Made out of necessity and for their creator's use and enjoyment, primitives are appealingly simple designs made without concern for correct proportions and fine details. There is little or no shading, no subtle gradations of color, in these early rugs because they were hooked with whatever leftover materials were on hand. The designs, inspired by the environment or by important events—the family home, a beloved pet, simple garden flowers, a patriotic motif—were drawn on the burlap and then gaily hooked, with a freedom and abandon present-day rug hookers should try to imitate.

Primitive rugs are characterized by striated backgrounds and abrupt changes in color. Although this was undoubtedly a direct result of the limited amounts of each material used, the different textures and colors give the rugs a more vital, intriguing appearance than evenly dyed, static colors could have produced. To imitate the streaked backgrounds of early rugs, you can hook in assorted, varied strips without further dyeing—although it remains a test of ingenuity to combine nondescript leftovers into a durable, attractive rug. If you prefer to do some dyeing, antique-black (see page 70) or spot-dyed (page 74) wools will give you a fluctuation similar to the early rugs. When dyeing for primitives, remember to cram *different* weights and weaves into the dye bath, stirring only occasionally; the resulting wool will be related but still vary enough to be effective. (Full dyeing instructions are in Chapter 8.)

Hooking was rarely done all in one direction in primitive rugs. Different areas of designs were often hooked in directional lines to emphasize shape and form—a straight road, for example, would be hooked horizontally; a sky, in a circular pattern. Frequently, hooking followed the contour of the center motif; then when one color ran out, the change was not as abrupt as it would have appeared with row-by-row horizontal hooking. The frequent change in direction added as much charm and interest to the primitive designs as the different textures and colors. Both directional hooking and fluctuating colors can be easily duplicated by today's rug hooker.

Special loosely woven burlap is recommended for adaptations of primitives because the wool must be cut wider than for other rugs—as wide as ¼ inch and even wider if the material is thin. With most materials, particularly tweeds, a width of ⅜″ is right. Before you cut all your wool, test a strip by hooking in a few loops; if it is hard to pull through the burlap, the wool is too wide.

Many adaptations of primitive rugs are available as patterns printed on burlap for rug hookers. At Craftsman Studio in Kennebunkport, Maine, we design and hand-screen hundreds of patterns on burlap—many of them primitive designs. If you want to design your own primitive rug, a visit to view the outstanding collections at Shelburne Museum, Shelburne, Vermont, Henry Ford Museum, Dearborn, Michigan, or Beauport, Gloucester, Massachusetts, will be very rewarding. Other valuable sources are the now out-of-print books by Stella Hay

Rex *(Choice Hooked Rugs* and *Practical Hooked Rugs)* and by William Winthrop Kent *(Hooked Rug Design, The Hooked Rug,* and *Rare Hooked Rugs).* Also see *American Hooked and Sewn Rugs* by Joel and Kate Kopp.

Adapting a primitive design you like is easy to do. (Transferring hints are in Chapter 5.) For example, the Mermaids rug, page 41, is copied from an antique rug given to me by a friend. I hooked my adaptation using new wool—some of the colors left over from other projects, some commercial swatches, and the rest dyed as needed. I cut some wool by machine and the rest by hand (about ¼″ wide). The vertical look of the letters, which could overly dominate this design, is offset by the wavy horizontal lines meant to suggest water. Spot-dyed swatches (Maxiswatch #201*) whose colors change and fluctuate from light to dark were perfect for the watery background. Because the letters were done with dark and medium-dark values, care was taken to keep the background behind them light (so that they would show up well). Similarly, the light tones of the mermaids' skin on faces and arms have darker tones behind them. The sly humor in the verse, the misspelling, and the casually drawn, uneven letters all add up to a rug of whimsical charm.

*Available from W. Cushing & Co.

In Old Nutfield (this primitive pattern screened on burlap is available from W. Cushing & Co.), Hallie Hall, with the help of her teacher Alice Beatty of Plainfield, New Jersey, created a very authentic-looking primitive (page 45). She used dull terracotta-red tweeds and old paisley (paisley must be cut by hand and about ½″ or ⅝″ wide, parallel with the long threads on the back) for the flowers and scrolls and green from her son's Marine Corps shirt for the leaves. If you don't have any paisley, then substitute colorful red and yellow tweeds or spot-dye plain wool; to produce her green you can use Cushing's Khaki Drab dye over a variety of medium-green flannels and tweeds. To duplicate her antique-black background, follow the directions on page 70. The resulting drab, streaked wools will produce a surprisingly effective and charming background, especially when hooked in swirling lines generally following the contours of the motifs. Mrs. Hall added a border to her rug, using all kinds of dull brownish tweeds mixed in with leftover blacks from her background. To separate the background and border, she used one line of gold and one line of paisley. The rug improves with age; it has been in use on the floor for over fifteen years, and its maker declares it is just now "coming into its own." There is a great deal of sentiment in a rug hooked with fabric from family garments, and its value (both sentimentally and monetarily) can only increase with the passing years.

Bengal Tiger. Origin unknown; the maker's initials (J.J.) are worked near the tiger's head. This tiger's charm certainly makes up for his anatomical imperfections. The rug was hooked with both cottons and wools, cut about ½″ wide and hooked about ½″ high. (Courtesy Shelburne Museum, Inc., Shelburne, Vermont)

Inspired by a primitive rug in Shelburne Museum, Vermont (page 37), Anne Ashworth hooked a tiger more amusing than menacing in appearance (page 44). Her color plan used tawny golds, rusty browns, and blacks for the tiger, set off by several dull gray-greens in the background and a border of tweed scallops with an antique-black background. The original tiger rug was hooked in the early 1800s by "J.J." (initials worked into rug). Both cotton and wool were used, cut about ½″ wide and hooked about ½″ high. The tiger was hooked in tans and browns, outlined in a reddish-brown; the huge four-leaf clovers in the corners, in a pinkish-tan outlined with a row of blue and then a row of white; and the background, in light olive.

Trotting ponies were a favorite subject for early rug hookers. The rug shown on the following page is an antique rug from Shelburne Museum. The pony was hooked in a

37

Trotting Pony. Origin unknown. The horizontal hooking of the striped background, emphasizing the direction in which the pony is trotting, is an important element in the design of this early rug. To capture so successfully the spirit of the pony—most likely a favorite pet—the rug hooker must have watched him closely many times.
(Courtesy Shelburne Museum, Inc., Shelburne, Vermont)

variety of dark browns with an off-white mane, tail, and socks; the sky, in many different blues; and the ground in greens. The colorful result conveys a spirited pony in motion. The sketch is of a similar primitive design available from W. Cushing & Co. in Maine. One very successful color scheme I have seen worked up had the horse hooked in pale grays, outlined in black with antique black mane, ears, tail, and hoofs. The leaves were done in bright autumn-colored tweeds and flannels, the ground area in a wide variety of leftover greens, and the sky in soft, pale greens, blues, and golds.

38

Below is a sketched adaptation of a rug called Cape May Primitive (Frontispiece). Cape May Primitive is regarded as an old rug—probably dating from the early nineteenth century—because it is hooked on homespun. The original has rich cranberry reds in the flowers, outlined with a variety of tans and browns. Its smaller flowers have cranberry reds and brown too as well as soft blues, and the leaves are hooked with mellow greens outlined with blacks. The design is so strong graphically that the rug is ageless in appearance.

39

Deer in the Woodland, page 133, hooked by Hallie Hall, was also inspired by a primitive rug. It was hooked with a variety of brown, tan, and rusty checks, as well as paisley strips. The light tones on the buck and doe were hooked with strips from a creamy-colored blanket. A variety of soft spot-dyed greens (also leftover greens from other rugs) appears in the ground areas and in the background of the border, as well as in the fanciful "tree" behind the doe's head. The radiating lines in this "tree" are hooked with paisley. Dark browns and blacks appear in tree trunks, buck's antlers and feet, in the foreground, and surrounding the paisley centers of the border motifs. Golds from light to dark were used in the large leaves at left, in the foliage of the tree at right, and outside the black line of the border motifs. Mrs. Hall cut a good deal of her materials by hand for this primitive rug.

Mermaids. Hooked by the author. The primitive design of a highly amusing antique rug—which may have been made by the "lonely sailor man" himself—was copied very closely onto a special loosely woven burlap. The wool—including spot-dyed wool, some commercial swatches, and assorted leftovers—was cut wider than usual (at least ¼" wide) by machine and by hand to achieve the primitive effect of the original.

41

**Spaniel Dogs. Origin unknown, 1875-1900. Two King Charles spaniels, primly seated on a cushion, pose for their portrait in wool. Note the ''dinner plate'' inner border and the naively drawn outer floral border. Fringe all around the edge is very unusual. Family pets are still the favorite subject of today's rug hookers.
(Courtesy Shelburne Museum, Inc., Shelburne, Vermont)**

The Spaniel rug, also from Shelburne Museum, is paired too with a sketch (page 40) of a pattern available from W. Cushing & Co. In the design adaptation, there are actually several backgrounds to fill in which requires a well-planned color scheme before getting started. The rug that the spaniel is reclining on is an ideal place to hook in leftover wools at random. The curving shapes in the oval frame can be treated like leaves, using tweed or spot-dyed wools to fill them in. If after hooking the dog, he seems to get lost in the design, just hook a line of dark brown around his outline.

Don't hesitate to use primitive designs as a wonderful opportunity to express yourself freely. When recreating an old design, use either the colors and techniques of the early craft or your own color preferences in your own individual way.

42

7 Cushing's Perfection Dyes

Cushing's Perfection Dyes are ideal for rug hooking, and have been used by generations of rug hookers. On the following pages, I have listed the proper names of these dyes, grouping them by color family. Opposite each family is a complementary color group. This means if you mix together two of the dyes, one from each group, they will gray and soften each other; it also means they can be used together harmoniously. For instance, if you have some bright fire-engine-red wool and you want to soften and gray it a little for use in a rug, then overdye it in a dye bath of a complementary color which you can see from the list would be Turquoise or Jade. The more Turquoise or Jade you use, the grayer your bright red wool will become. Or suppose you have some brilliant blue wool that you would like to use up but it is just too bright. Overdye it in one of the complements of blue: Apricot or Orange. The more Apricot or Orange you use in the dye pot, the grayer your brilliant blue will become.

Bengal Tiger. Hooked by Anne Ashworth. This design was adapted from an antique rug (Chapter 6) now at the Shelburne Museum. To imitate the primitive look of the original, Mrs. Ashworth used the method of the earliest rug hookers: she hooked the background following the general contour of the tiger, also hooking occasional random shapes and then filling them in. Backgrounds hooked in this way are much more interesting than straight, unvarying rows of horizontal hooking.
Illustrated on color plate D.

Opposite page, top: Old Nutfield. Hooked by Hallie Hall. In this rug adapted from an antique rug, mostly old wool was used. More than any other handcraft, except perhaps for quilting, rug hooking recycles otherwise worthless scraps and worn-out clothing into useful products, often of heirloom quality. This rug includes wool from the Marine Corps uniform of Mrs. Hall's son and a torn paisley shawl cut into strips by hand.
Illustrated on color plate D.

Opposite page, bottom: Lions in a Desert Scene. This nineteenth-century rug is based—very remotely—on a Frost pattern, which included only the lion. The fantastic setting of red palm trees proves that Frost patterns were not inhibiting to the imaginative. (Collection Betty Sterling)
Shown in color on inside front cover.

Of course this method works in reverse too. Say you have some bright orange wool. You could soften and gray it by overdyeing it in one of the dyes listed in the Blue family, such as Aqualon Blue. Or if you have some brilliant turquoise wool, overdye it in a dye listed in the Red family, such as Old Rose or Scarlet.

When in doubt, experiment on small samples of wool. (Be sure to read Chapter 10 on overdyeing.) Don't forget to tag your dyed wool samples or to glue the samples in a notebook with an explanation. You will refer back to your notes many times in future rug planning. By experimenting you will gain a better understanding of color and be able to make it work for you in your hooked rugs. For example, the same pattern, worked in two different color schemes, is illustrated on page 48. One rug was hooked in traditional, muted crewel colors; the other, in black, white, and grays, giving it the most modern of appearances.

RED FAMILY		BLUE-GREEN FAMILY
Old Rose		
Crimson		
Scarlet		Jade Green
Turkey Red	Complements	Turquoise
Cardinal		
Maroon		
Dark Brown		

RED—YELLOW-RED FAMILY		BLUE-GREEN—BLUE FAMILY
Coral		
Wood Rose		
Salmon		
Terra Cotta	Complements	Turquoise Blue
Egyptian Red		Peacock
Brown		
Mahogany		

46

YELLOW-RED FAMILY

BLUE FAMILY

Champagne
Peach
Tan   Baby Blue
Taupe   Complements   Aqua
Light Brown   Robin's Egg Blue
Medium Brown
Apricot
Orange
Rust
Golden Brown
Seal Brown
Mummy Brown
Spice Brown
Brown Rust

YELLOW-RED—YELLOW
FAMILY

BLUE-PURPLE—BLUE
FAMILY

Old Ivory
Ecru
Aqualon Yellow   Sky Blue
Maize   Complements
Yellow
Buttercup Yellow
Gold
Old Gold
Nugget Gold

YELLOW FAMILY

PURPLE-BLUE FAMILY

Canary   Light Blue
Bronze   Complements   Copenhagen Blue
Khaki   Blue
Lemon   Navy Blue

YELLOW—GREEN-YELLOW
FAMILY

PURPLE-BLUE—PURPLE
FAMILY

Khaki Drab   Royal Blue
Chartreuse   Complements

47

Right: Samplers are an excellent way for beginning rug hookers to learn how different fabrics—tweed, checks, plaids, paisley—look when hooked into the burlap foundation.
Illustrated on color plate H.

Below: Seventeenth Century. Designed by the author, the black and white rug was hooked by Milda Berry, the multicolored rug by Polly Merrill. The same pattern based on crewel work is done in two color schemes with startlingly different results. The one in black and white has a very contemporary look; the other, in the muted colors of seventeenth-century crewel, has a more traditional feeling.
Illustrated on color plate B.

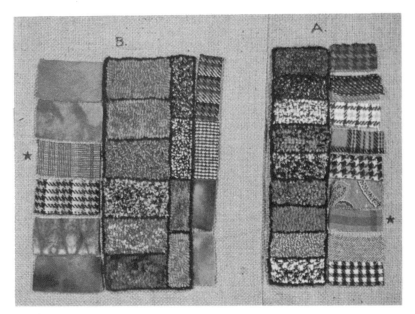

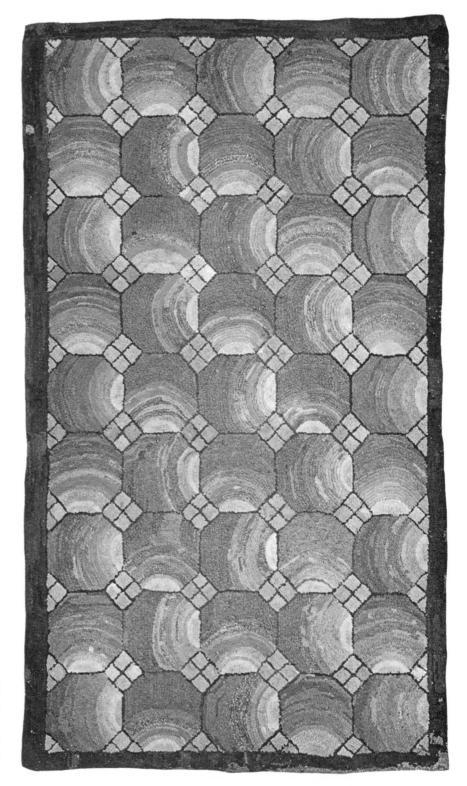

This handsome geometric, a nineteenth-century rug from "Beauport," Gloucester, Massachusetts, is worked in a very subtle palette of cool browns. A completely different effect could be obtained by working the same design in bold colors.

49

GREEN-YELLOW FAMILY

Ocean Green
Olive Green   Complements
Bronze Green
Bright Green

**GREEN-YELLOW—GREEN
FAMILY**

Nile Green
Aqua Green   Complements
Mint Green
Hunter Green

GREEN FAMILY

Silver Gray-Green
Myrtle Green   Complements

GREEN—BLUE-GREEN FAMILY

Reseda Green
Green   Complements
Dark Green
Turquoise Green

PURPLE FAMILY

Lavender
Violet
Bright Purple
Purple

**PURPLE—RED-PURPLE
FAMILY**

Orchid
Plum

RED-PURPLE FAMILY

Aqualon Wine
Magenta
Wine
Garnet
Mulberry
Burgundy
Red Grape

**RED-PURPLE—RED
FAMILY**

Aqualon Pink
Pink
Wild Rose
Rose
Strawberry
Cherry
American Beauty
Rose Pink

On the Cushing's Perfection Dye color card, a valuable aid for every serious rug hooker, the color shown is approximately what you will get over white wool at the ratio of one package of

50

dye to one pound of wool. If you dye over a colored wool, the result, of course, will be different. For instance, Scarlet dye over yellow wool will produce orange wool (see Chapter 10 on overdyeing). Remember to use less of the darker colors when using them to gray or soften a complementary color.

It is extremely helpful to own a set of small colored wool swatches, one for each Cushing's dye. Certainly every hooking teacher should own one. A good way for an individual to acquire such a set at reasonable cost is for a hooking group to cooperate in dyeing a whole set, dividing the results among themselves. If there are ten in your group, you could each take about ten dyes (less since there are 95 Cushing's dyes) and dye a swatch of each dye. Then divide each swatch into ten smaller swatches and give one to each member of your group. The planning of rugs will be so much simpler with this aid. You can use the swatches to match or harmonize with existing colors in your rooms, such as walls, draperies, and upholstered furniture, and, most important, to develop original color schemes.

Monterey Tile. Designed and hooked by the author. This simple geometric design, an ideal project for intermediate rug hookers, can be worked in bright, vibrant colors or, for an entirely different effect, in muted pastels. Illustrated on color plate H.

Right: detail. The swatches show the surprisingly few colors used to work this design. Just five values of rust-red and three blues are accented with a green and three values of gold. Illustrated on color plate H.

Right: Fleur de Lis. Designed and hooked by the author. A single motif can produce a stunning repeat pattern, even in a very large rug—particularly when combined, as it is here, with a marbleized background. To dye wool for a mottled effect, the wool is crowded into the dye pan, and the dye bath is stirred infrequently.

Below: Chinese Moth window valance, detail. Designed by the author, hooked by Polly Merrill. Rug hookers frequently overlook many ideal uses for their craft; window valances, for example, are a satisfying project for a usually prominent place. In this valance, blue and white predominate, but there are touches of related greens and contrasting bittersweet. The moth in Chinese design symbolizes longevity and good tidings. Illustrated on color plate F.

8 Dyeing Methods

Dyeing wool for hooking projects is such a rewarding experience that it is a pity some rug hookers avoid it, mistakenly believing that it is a complicated and difficult process. Nothing could be further from the truth. It is easy and fun with the added advantage of keeping the cost of the craft to a minimum. Perhaps the most important reason for dyeing your own wool is simply that rugs hooked with home-dyed wool strips are more beautiful and interesting than those rugs made *exclusively* with commercially dyed swatches and backgrounds.

There is no one correct way to dye. Like good cooks, we develop our own individual way of doing it, always keeping within the framework of a few basic rules.

The color is brought into contact with the wool by using water, and when that takes place we use heat and salt *or* vinegar to make the color permanent. When I say "permanent" I use the word with reservations because the best and most carefully dyed rug will fade if left in strong sunlight too often and too long. While salt and vinegar are being mentioned, let me stress that each is equally effective—but with an important difference: salt will soften and gray the color slightly; vinegar will sharpen and brighten the color slightly. (Fix this difference in your mind—you will find it a useful piece of information.)

Suppose you are dyeing a soft gold background. You are afraid that it might be a little too bright. Very well . . . use *salt* to soften and gray the color.

Or, perhaps you think that the rose-pink you are dyeing for flowers could be just a little brighter. Use *vinegar* to brighten it.

Note: Always wear rubber gloves and work in a well-ventilated area when dyeing. Do not use cooking pots, but keep separate dye pots, using them for dyeing only.

EASY DIP-DYEING

Easy dip-dyeing is a creative way to get those important subtle "off" shades that will put the unmistakable stamp of originality on your rugs. I find that more and more of my pupils prefer to dye their own swatches, using the dip-dye method. It is also my favorite, being the simplest and quickest method. Another important advantage is the way the shading is dyed into the wool strip, ready to be hooked in almost automatically.

The things you will need are easy to assemble.

1. Cushing's Perfection Dyes
   A good basic set to order is as follows:

Cardinal	Reseda Green	Bronze Green
Old Gold	Wild Rose	Aqualon Blue
Navy	Bright Purple	Wine
Turquoise Green	Black	Medium Brown
		Golden Brown
		Maize

2. white enamel pan, 2- or 3-quart capacity
3. small white enamel pan (for mixing the dyes)

Cape Shore Crewel. Designed by the author, hooked by Mary Langzettel. A fanciful version of the ever-popular tree-of-life motif is enjoyable to design and to work. Any color scheme will work; the flowers, in particular, are an excellent place to use up leftover wool. The background of this design, done in traditional ivory, is slightly striated for additional interest.
Illustrated on color plate F.

4. flat white enamel pan, about 9″ × 12″ (or longer)
5. 6 pieces of white wool flannel
   1 piece of medium-gray flannel
   1 piece of medium-green flannel
   All about 9″ × 12″ or approximately the same size as your flat
   pan.
6. white paper towels
7. white vinegar
8. aluminum foil
9. **rubber gloves**
10. **bleach**
11. **dishwashing liquid**

Presoak the pieces of wool for a few minutes in hot water and 1 tablespoon dishwashing liquid. The dishwashing liquid helps water to soak the wool thoroughly and enables the dye to penetrate properly.

The following directions will give you some beautiful, richly shaded pieces of wool particularly useful for flowers. This kind of dyeing works well for leaves too; just substitute Reseda Green or one of the other green dyes for the Wild Rose dye.

Before starting, read the directions over once or twice to understand the entire process.

Put some newspapers on your countertop to make cleaning up easy.

Open the package of Wild Rose dye and put ¼ teaspoon of it in the small enamel pan. Then add ½ cup boiling water and stir thoroughly, preferably over heat to help dissolve the tiny particles of dye. This is called the dye solution.

In the 3-quart pan put *about* 1½ quarts of water and bring the water to a boil. Add to it 2 tablespoons of vinegar and 1 teaspoon of the Wild Rose dye solution. This is called the dye bath.

Keep heat on high so that the dye bath is continuously boiling hard.

Now put on your rubber gloves, and holding a wet piece of white wool by one end, dip the wool—up to about 3 inches from the bottom of the piece—in the boiling dye bath. (Don't hold it still or a line will form. Keep it moving up and down

57

going just slightly deeper each time.) You will see that the dye will begin to penetrate the immersed end of the wool and the water will start to clear. As soon as this begins to happen, start dipping deeper and deeper. By the time the dye bath is almost clear you can dip the wool *all* the way in for a second or two (the rubber gloves will protect your fingers), and the top end will take on a tint of pink.

You may add another ¼ teaspoon or more of the dye solution to the dye bath if you need more color toward the top end, and dip as before. You will see that your piece of wool is now shaded from pink at the top to deep rose at the bottom.

Remember to keep the heat on high so that the water returns to a hard boil (it will tend to go off the boil in the dipping process).

Now lay your lovely shaded piece of wool *flat* in the 9″ × 12″ pan and repeat the process with the other pieces of wool, adding more boiling water from time to time as it tends to boil away, and using 1 teaspoon (or more) of dye solution and about ½ teaspoon of vinegar for each succeeding piece of wool.

Finally, dye the medium-gray wool and medium-green wool, dipping in the Wild Rose dye bath, using about 2 teaspoons of dye solution for the gray piece and about 3 teaspoons of dye solution for the green piece. These will give you some darker, duller shades, useful for the inside petals of tulips, roses, and other flowers.

As each piece of wool is dyed, lay it carefully on top of the other dyed pieces, dark end on top of dark end and light end on top of light end. Put the darker shades which were dyed over the gray and green wool at the bottom of the pile with one or two white paper towels separating them from the lighter pieces. (Regarding the paper towels, don't make the same mistake I once made and use colored paper towels. The yellow came out of the towels and went into my dyed strips, although it wasn't as bad as it could have been because I was dip-dyeing some green for leaves and the yellow harmonized very well!)

Throw out the dye bath, and if the sides of the pan are stained from the dye, bleach them out and rinse well.

The leftover dye solution may be safely stored in a jar.

(Purchase an inexpensive box of gummed labels and write the name of the dye on the jar.)

To set the color, mix ¼ cup vinegar with 2 cups hot water. Gently pour enough of this solution over your dyed pieces of wool to make them thoroughly moist but not "swimming." If you add too much water, some of the dye might bleed out of the dark ends and travel through the water to spoil the light ends, so be careful to add just enough to have them all *very moist,* but no more. (Just wet enough so that they don't dry out in the oven.)

Cover the pan tightly with foil and put it in a 300° oven for one hour. After taking the pan out of the oven, rinse the wool well. It can be dried either outdoors or in the dryer, warm setting.

To use these pieces, cut them lengthwise so that one end of the strip is light, gradually darkening to the other end. Please don't make the mistake of cutting them all up at once. It is much better to cut just a few strips at a time as they are needed. The colors are easier to see. If at times you need more of a certain shade, then tear your wool across instead of lengthwise to get more of the needed shade. It is surprising how the odd bits and pieces of lights and darks get used up.

A strip of wool which is 12 inches long will measure, when hooked in, about 4 inches. This is ideal if the petal or leaf you want to hook is 4 inches long. But suppose the petal or leaf is only 2 inches long. Then simply hook in rows of 2 stitches as in Figure 21. You will still achieve the lovely subtle shading, but you will use up the strip twice as quickly. It is amazing how quickly you learn tricks like this when using dip-dyed wools.

Animals and birds are much easier to hook by using dip-dyed wools. Later on in this chapter, you will find color suggestions for these. Have color pictures to guide you and you will see where the shadows, medium shades, and highlights should go.

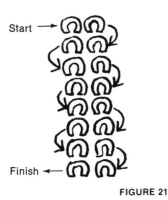

Start →

Finish ←

FIGURE 21

Dip-dyeing with More than One Color

I urge you to try dip-dyeing with two colors (after you have mastered dyeing with one color)—you will be delighted

59

with the results. For instance, after dipping in the Wild Rose dye, and before you set the colors in the oven, the dyed pieces can be rinsed in clear water and then overdyed part way up the strip in another color such as Gold dye. After you have dipped the pieces in the second dye, the colors should be set in the oven as before. This method will give you some very rich colors with which to work.

I hope that you will be inspired to try other colors. Dip-dyeing—once you have mastered the few basic rules—is fun to do and the results are very impressive. You will find that shading from dark to light, or from one color to another color, will be easiest with dip-dyed strips.

Below are some suggested formulas and their possible uses. Try some of your own ideas too. Dip over already colored wools—in addition to white—to achieve some interesting results.

ROSE LEAVES

> Dip first in Bronze Green, then in weak Mahogany
> Dip first in Myrtle Green, then in weak Wild Rose
> Dip first in Reseda Green, then in weak Khaki Drab

LEAVES

> Dip first in Aqualon Blue, then in Bronze Green
> Dip first in Reseda Green, then in weak Turquoise Blue
> Dip first in Chartreuse, then in Olive Green
> Dip first in Silver Gray-green, then in weak Aqualon Wine
> Dip first in Bronze Green, then in weak Light Blue
> Dip first in Brown Rust, then in Bronze Green

ROSES and other FLOWERS

> Dip first in ½ Cherry and ½ Spice Brown mixed together, then in ¼ Cherry and ¾ Spice Brown mixed together
> Dip first in Orchid, then in Maroon
> Dip first in Gold, then in Terra Cotta
> Dip first in Turkey Red, then in Wine
> Dip first in ½ Wine and ½ Egyptian Red mixed together, then in Dark Green

PANSIES and TULIPS and IRIS

Dip first in Coral, then in Wine
Dip first in Lavender, then in Wine
Dip first in Copenhagen Blue, then in Orange
Dip first in Bright Purple, then in Coral
Dip first in Buttercup Yellow, then in Violet
Dip first in Aqualon Blue, then in Mulberry
Dip first in Aqualon Wine, then in Black
Dip first in Mummy Brown, then in Dark Brown
Dip first in Wild Rose, then in Gold

BLUE FLOWERS (Soft!)

Dip first in Silver Gray, then in weak Navy
Dip white- or peach-colored wool in Aqua, then in weak Blue

DOGWOOD

Dip first in Tan, then in weak Aqualon Pink

MORNING GLORIES

Dip first in Turquoise Blue, then in weak Bright Purple

DAFFODILS

Dip first in Old Gold, then in weak Mummy Brown

LILIES

Dip first in Old Ivory, then in weak Rust
Dip first in Old Ivory, then in weak Bronze Green

SQUIRREL

Dip first in Silver Gray, then in Medium Brown

SIAMESE CAT

Dip first in Ecru, then in Seal Brown

GRAY CAT

Dip in Dark Gray. Use white and tan wool.

GINGER CAT

Dip in Mummy Brown. Use white, yellow, brown, and pale blue wool.

GRAY HORSE

Dip in Silver Gray or Dark Gray. Use white, tan, and gray wool.

BAY HORSE

Dip in ½ Golden Brown and ½ Spice Brown mixed together

CHESTNUT HORSE

Dip in ½ Yellow, ¼ Golden Brown, and ¼ Brown Rust mixed together. Use white and pale blue wool.

PALAMINO HORSE

Dip in ½ Old Ivory and ½ Champagne mixed together

CHICKADEES

WINGS: Dip in Silver Gray
BREAST: Dip in Maize, then in weak Mummy Brown

CARDINALS

Dip in Turkey Red, then in weak Dark Brown

ROBINS

WINGS and HEAD: Dip in Dark Gray, then in Seal Brown
BREAST: Dip in Coral using pale blue or gray wool

Keep samples of your dyeing and note the dyes used and the wool that was dyed over for future reference.

GRADATION DYEING

Now we are going to dye a batch called "gradation." This will give you a series of shades of one color, going from light to dark. While the dip-dyed swatches are my favorites, gradation swatches are useful and favored by many rug hookers.

Chances are you will have most of the equipment you will need already in the house.

1. Small enamel pan in which to mix the dye
2. Two white enamel pans with covers (3- or 4-quart capacity)
3. Ordinary kitchen measuring spoons (or dye-measuring spoons)
4. White vinegar
5. Bleach (to remove the dye stains from pans)
6. Notebook (in which to record formulas and results)
7. White wool flannel, 7 pieces, each about 9″ × 12″, and 2 extra pieces, same size, one pale green and one tan
8. Cushing's dyes (see page 55 on basic set to order)
9. Dishwashing liquid
10. Rubber gloves

The following directions will give you nine beautiful shades for roses or other flowers. Do *not* follow directions on the dye packages, except of course for dyeing garments, etc.; for rug hooking, the dyeing does not have to be even—in fact, a fluctuation in color or mottled appearance is very desirable.

Spread a newspaper on your countertop to catch stray specks of dye (if you *should* get dye accidentally on counters it will easily clean off).

Carefully open package of Wine dye and put 1 level teaspoon of it into the small enamel pan, add 1 cup boiling water, and let it simmer on the stove for a minute or two, stirring well to dissolve completely the tiny particles of dye. This is the dye solution.

Soak wool pieces in hot water and 1 tablespoon of dishwashing liquid for a few minutes (rinsing is not necessary).

In 4-quart pan, put about 2 quarts of hot water, and place the pan on high heat. This is the dye bath.

Next, put ½ teaspoon of dye solution and 2 tablespoons of vinegar into the dye bath. Put in 1 piece of the wet wool, stir with a fork, bring to a boil, and then simmer for 20 minutes. Remove the wool. This is your lightest shade or "highlight."

For the second shade, put 1 teaspoon of dye solution into the dye bath, and add 1 teaspoon of vinegar and another strip of wool. Stir, boil, then simmer 20 minutes. Remove the wool. Rinse in cold water and compare with the first shade. There should be a slight but perceptible difference in shade.

Repeat, adding 2 teaspoons of dye solution for the third shade. Simmer 20 minutes. Remove, rinse, and compare as before. Repeat, adding 1 tablespoon of dye solution for the fourth shade. Simmer 30 minutes, remove, etc. (Note: 20 minutes "cooking" time is enough for light tints, but longer time is needed for the darker shades.)

If necessary, add more water to the dye bath, since it tends to boil away. Just make sure that there is enough water to comfortably hold the wool.

Repeat the same process with the fifth piece of wool, adding 2 tablespoons of dye solution and 1 tablespoon of vinegar, simmering 30 minutes.

Repeat with the sixth piece of wool, adding 3½ tablespoons of dye solution, simmering 30 minutes.

Now add the remainder of the dye solution and the seventh piece of wool; after it has come to a boil, throw in the two extra pieces of wool (presoaked in dishwashing liquid). These will give you some delightful "off" shades useful for shadows in flowers or veins in leaves. Let the three pieces of wool simmer for 30 minutes, then remove the odd pieces. Add to the remaining piece of wool some dry Reseda Green dye (just a few specks) to help darken it. (Note: Reseda Green is a near complement of Wine—see page 46—and it will gray this last piece.) Simmer 15 minutes more.

Now, rinse all your wool pieces well, and dry either outdoors or in the dryer at the warm setting.

Larger amounts of wool can be dyed at a time. Just use a larger pan and proportionately larger amounts of wools and dyes.

I love to arrange the dyed wool in a pile from light to dark. I always feel a thrill of achievement and anticipation as I admire their graduated harmony.

For different effects, follow the directions for gradation dyeing, but instead of dyeing over white wool, try dyeing over pastel-colored wools. By using the Wild Rose dye over blue wool and yellow wool as well as the white, you will have three decidedly different swatches to use in the same rug, yet they will be related in a delightful way. Your rugs will thus gain character and individuality.

I urge you to train your eye when dyeing. If, when following the directions, you think that the gradation is not as smooth as you would like, then add a little more dye solution to the too-pale shade. (Just add a little at a time though—it is easier to add more than it is to take it out.)

You will find that the water clears when dyeing light shades. But as you dye the darker shades the water is not so likely to clear. Be cautious about adding more dye at this stage—while the dye bath simmers, the wool is likely to continue absorbing some of the dye that is already present.

For light shades, simmering 20 minutes is enough. For darker shades, simmer at least 30 minutes. If you cannot seem to get dark shades dark enough, add a few specks of a complementary dye (see list on page 46) or a tiny bit of Black.

When comparing dark shades, it is difficult to tell them apart when they are soaking wet. Wring out small pieces of them, and then it is easy to compare them. (I wring the pieces out in an old towel.)

The amount of water in a dye bath is not important, as long as the wool is accommodated comfortably. What is important, is the proportion of *dye* to the amount of *wool* present. The water is there simply to bring them together.

ONION-SKIN DYEING

Onion-skin dyeing is fun to do and the results are delightful. Keep a bag of these dyed wools by your hooking frame, and you will use them in all your projects.

Save the dry outer skins of yellow onions (your produce man at the supermarket will gladly give you some if you don't eat many onions). Now gather together an assortment of colored wools, new or used, in all sorts of odd sizes, small pieces or long strips. The colors can be red, rose, orange, yellow, tan, green, blue, gray, lavender, and some small checks and tweeds if you have them. Soak the wools for a minute or two in dishwashing liquid in warm water. Then arrange them casually in layers in an enamel pan (they don't even have to be put in flat—be *very casual* about it), but *between each layer* throw in a handful of the dry onion skins and sprinkle the skins with ½ tablespoon of salt. Let the pile build up to within 2 or 3 inches of the top of the pan, then cover with boiling water. Let simmer *without stirring* for 45 minutes to release the color; then rinse well and dry.

The warm, soft orangy-tan color from the skins acts as a common denominator and goes into and softens all the colors. Also, some of the color from the various wools "bleeds" and goes into the other colors, and you literally end up with a rainbow of soft hues.

As an alternative, you could use equal parts of Ecru and Champagne mixed together to achieve similar results.

I kept a bag full of these lovely onion-skin-dyed scraps available at all times in our YWCA hooking class, and as it got low, one or another of my pupils donated pieces of her own onion-skin dyeing. Then everyone felt free to help themselves to whatever odd color they needed as an accent.

9 Dyeing Backgrounds

In Chapter 4 you will find information on hooking backgrounds; now I am going to give you some specific instructions on how to dye the wool for them. You will need a large enamel pan, preferably white, with a cover.

MOTTLED

My own preference is for the slightly fluctuating or marbleized backgrounds found in antique hooked rugs. A fluctuating background, besides being beautiful, is the most practical because it is slow to show dust and soil marks. To achieve this appearance we need unevenly dyed wool.

The pan I use is large enough to accommodate one pound of wool. For a large rug, I like to dye just one pound, then do another when I see my supply is running low, so it is essential to have a record of what dye I used and how much. In my notebook I glue a sample of the wool I dyed over, the name of the dye used, and the proportion of dye solution mixed with water (for example: 1 teaspoon Old Ivory to 1 cup boiling water), the amount of that dye solution used for 1 yard of white wool, and a sample of the dyed wool. Due to many factors, however, it is almost impossible to match exactly an earlier dye lot; but the slight variation you will end up with is a highly desirable feature in a handcrafted rug.

To get the uneven dyeing effect I like, I am careful to *crowd* the wool somewhat into the pan. For 1 pound of wool, I add ½ cup salt and let it simmer ¾ hour to make sure the heat has penetrated to the center of the pan. (Another way to get uneven dyeing is to have the water near to the boiling point and the salt in the water *before* putting in the wool.)

PLAIN

Now, suppose you do want your background to be evenly colored, not mottled. Here are a few tips to help you.

Use plenty of water and do not crowd wool in the pan. Put wool in dye bath well before the water reaches the boiling point and stir constantly until it starts to simmer. Let it simmer 15 minutes, stirring often, remove from heat, *then* add salt and simmer 15 minutes more (30 minutes if you are dyeing a dark color).

Generally speaking, it is best to use salt as the setting agent for backgrounds, because (remember?) it will soften the color, and we want the wool for *back*grounds as the name implies. The background must not compete with the design for attention. (There are exceptions to this rule, as in some geometric rugs and contemporary designs where the backgrounds are more important in the overall scheme.)

It's your decision whether to dye your wool evenly or unevenly. Remember, wet wool will dry one shade lighter.

There are many more lovely backgrounds to be obtained from Cushing's dyes. This partial list is only to guide you.

You will notice I suggest several different wools to overdye. You could use just one of the suggested wools if you happen to have a lot of it, or if it suits you better, use all the wools together in the same dye pot. The dye will unify them into a single color, but they will have that slight difference from each other which is so intriguing when hooked in.

LIGHT BACKGROUNDS

DYE	COLOR OF WOOL	RESULT
weak Silver Gray-green	pale gray or off-white	soft green
weak Reseda Green	oatmeal or off-white	soft gray-green
weak Green	pale pink or off-white	soft bluish-green
weak Bronze Green	off-white or ivory	yellowish-green
Khaki Drab	pale gray or off-white	dull yellowish drab
Old Ivory	white or off-white	soft brown-gold
Champagne	oatmeal or off-white	warm orangy tint
Old Gold	white or off-white	soft gold
weak Golden Brown	white or off-white	yellowish beige
Taupe	pale gray, white, or off-white	warm gray-beige
weak Mahogany	off-white or pale green	soft rosy-beige
weak Egyptian Red	off-white, gray, or oatmeal	brick-beige
weak Wine	off-white or gray	soft grayed pink
weak Black	off-white or pale peach	"Williamsburg" gray-blue
weak Bright Purple	off-white or ivory	soft grayed purple
weak Plum	off-white or gray	soft rosy-purple
Aqua	off-white or gray	very soft blue

DARK BACKGROUNDS

DYE	COLOR OF WOOL	RESULT
medium-strength Black	green, orange, blue, or gray	grayed green-blue
Maroon	rose, green, aqua, or gray	dull red
Wine	rose, green, aqua, or gray	rich wine
Mahogany	rose, green, aqua, or gray	brown-red
Mulberry	rose, aqua, or gray	purplish wine
Dark Brown	rose, blue-green, or gray	rich red-brown
Reseda Green	rose, green, or gray	grayed green
Bronze Green	pale lavender, green, or gray	rich yellow-green
Dark Green	rose, green, or gray	rich evergreen
Golden Brown	blue, gray, yellow, or green	glowing brown

(NOTE: good with pine & maple furniture)

Spice Brown	rose, blue, green, or gray	dark, dull yet spicy brown
1 part Cherry and 3 parts Spice Brown	purple	eggplant color

For a mottled background, remember to crowd the wool in the dye pot just a little, so that it won't take the dye too evenly, although you should still stir it occasionally. Have the water cover the wool and use about ½ cup uniodized salt to set the colors. Simmer about 45 minutes. Don't forget to rinse the wool thoroughly. (I use my washing machine.) Dry outdoors or in a dryer, warm setting.

METHODS OF DYEING ANTIQUE BLACK

Method #1. Gather all kinds of harshly colored wools together, such as reds, blues, kelly greens, purples, yellows, checks, and plaids—this is a good way to use up unwanted odds and ends—and overdye them with Dark Green for a greenish-black result. Or use *medium-strength* black (be careful not to add too much) for bluish-black wool, or use equal parts of Dark Green and Burgundy for another shade of "black" wool. The results will be a variety of shades, and you should cut and mix them all together to hook in at random. I think you will be intrigued and pleased when you see how the different shades look when hooked in.

Method #2. If you have some bright red wool you want to use up, overdye it with Dark Green. Or if you have a lot of bright kelly green (or different shades of green) wool, overdye in Mahogany or Dark Brown, adding a small amount of Black if the fabric doesn't get dark enough. If you are in doubt, it is easier to tell if you wring out a small piece and examine it in a good light. Remember, you are aiming for an *off*-black.

I hope you can see by now that dyeing is easy and not even messy. With the simple directions I have given for dyeing gradations and backgrounds, you will be able to go ahead and make beautiful rugs!

10 Dyeing Remedies

OVERDYEING

No harsh, ugly-colored wool ever need be thrown away—there are always several dyes that can change an undesirable color into a lovely, unexpected "off" shade. Your growing experience with dyes and occasional experimentation with them will guide you to successful remedies for colored wools that would otherwise be worthless to you.

Below are some suggestions for overdyeing. I urge you to do a little experimenting, for by doing so you will discover exceedingly beautiful shades—shades that possibly you never knew existed.

The more dye you use, the deeper will be the overdyeing. You will quickly learn how much to use. Also, it will be affected by how dark or how bright the wool is you are dyeing over.

71

Kelly green wool	overdyed in	Mahogany
Kelly green wool	overdyed in	Navy Blue
Dark green wool	overdyed in	Wine
Dark green wool	overdyed in	Terra Cotta
Bright blue wool	overdyed in	Golden Brown
Bright blue wool	overdyed in	Old Gold
Scarlet wool	overdyed in	Jade
Bright yellow wool	overdyed in	Purple
Bright yellow wool	overdyed in	Magenta
Sky blue wool	overdyed in	Champagne
Rose wool	overdyed in	Turquoise-green
Purple wool	overdyed in	Khaki

Overdyeing for Flowers, Leaves, and Scrolls

The following are suggestions only to open your eyes to the infinite possibilities before you.

Leaves: Yellow wool can be overdyed using Turquoise-green, Khaki Drab, or Reseda Green. Harsh green wool can be softened for leaves, using Old Gold, Aqualon Yellow, or Mahogany. For blue wool you might try Olive Green or Bronze or, in the case of light blue wool, Ecru.

Flowers: Blue wool, which must not be used in bright shades for flowers or they will seem to "jump" out of the rug, can be made acceptable by overdyeing in Peach or Apricot or Silver Gray. Too-bright yellow wool, also undesirable, can be toned down by overdyeing it in weak solutions of Plum, Reseda Green, Wine, or Orchid.

Bright red wool can be dyed for gorgeous deep red roses if you dip-dye or dye graduated shades as directed, using Dark Brown, Burgundy, Dark Green, or Black.

Scrolls: Scrolls are usually kept in softer colors than the flowers they surround. Here are a few suggestions. Lavender wool can be softened by overdyeing in Bronze or Khaki (good for flowers too). Bright pink wool can be toned down by overdyeing in weak Reseda Green or Myrtle; orange wool, by overdyeing in weak Black, Aqualon Blue, or Aqua.

72

I could go on and on, as I look over my wool samples resulting from years of experimenting. Do try combinations for yourself and make notes of the results. You will refer to them again and again, and best of all, a whole new world of fascinating hues and shades will open up before your dazzled eyes!

Flower Centers: Make up a bundle of small black and white or brown and white checked wools, some tweeds and mixtures, and also some blue, yellow, and lilac wools, and soak them all in detergent for a few minutes, using hot water. Dye half of your bundle in a fairly strong dye bath using Chartreuse and dye the other half in a fairly strong dye bath using Gold. This will give you a good variety of flower centers, and they will add much interest and sparkle to your flowers.

REMOVING COLOR

Another way to get delightful colors is to take some color out of your wool by simmering (*not* boiling) the wool in a generous pan of water to which has been added a few tablespoons of ammonia or detergent. Let the wool just barely simmer for a minute or two; most times you will be amazed at what comes out. Then, if you would like more color removed, empty the water out and start again with fresh water and more ammonia, etc. The reason I caution you against boiling is because it tends to weaken the material. When you are satisfied that enough color has been removed, *rinse well*, especially if you used ammonia. You may be so pleased with the result, that you will decide to use it "as is"; if so, then it is advisable to set the color by simmering ½ hour in a salt or vinegar bath. (Remember the rule: salt grays the color slightly, vinegar brightens it slightly — so use your own judgement.) Or you may decide to overdye the wool.

Black wool simmered in ammonia water, I have found, will often emerge a soft grayed blue. Lovely!

73

11 Fashion Fabric Spot-dyeing

This method of spot-dyeing truly creates fashion fabrics. The delightful results have inspired many rug hookers to use the dyed fabric for a dress, pair of pants, or poncho—always with the thrifty thought that when the garment is worn out or no longer in style, it can be cut up and hooked into a rug. There is a fashionable boutique in our town whose owner follows these directions and makes long skirts with the spot-dyed wool, asking and getting a considerable price for them.

Large pieces of wool—up to two yards of 54-inch-wide fabric—can be dyed at a time using this method. The advantages of dyeing such large amounts of wool at one time are immediately apparent to the seasoned rug hooker.

It is safe to say that you cannot make a mistake with this spot-dyeing. The colors blend into delightful "off" shades that are constantly a surprise, but because they are related to the dyes used, the effect is always harmonious. Spot-dyed wool makes a fantastically beautiful background—the color subtly changing and fluctuating as in marble or malachite. Hook it in straight lines for one effect, and in wavy lines for another.

You will need:

> 1½ yards 54-inch-wide flannel. The color can be off-white, beige, or any pastel color
> Cushing's Perfection Dye: one package each of Old Rose, Yellow, and Copenhagen Blue
> Dishwashing liquid
> A bowl or saucepan big enough to hold 6 cups water
> Two smaller bowls or pans
> One large flat pan, the bigger the better (mine came from a restaurant supply store—Wearever Model #5321, size 16″ × 24″). Or use the largest roasting pan you can find.
> 1 cup uniodized salt
> Some heavy-duty aluminum foil
> Rubber gloves

Directions

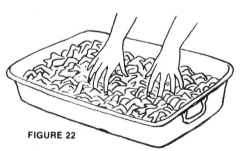

FIGURE 22

Fill the kitchen sink ¾ full of warm water; add 2 tablespoons of dishwashing liquid. Put in the wool and let it soak for a few minutes, then pull the stopper in the sink and let the water drain out. While the wool is draining, prepare the dye solutions.

In the large bowl or pan empty the Old Rose dye, add 6 cups of boiling water, and stir thoroughly. This is called the main color.

In one of the smaller pans empty the Yellow dye, add 3 cups of boiling water, and stir thoroughly. This is called the second color.

In the other smaller pan, put ¼ teaspoon Copenhagen Blue dye, add 1 cup of boiling water, and stir thoroughly. This is called the accent color.

Now you will begin to have fun!

Take the wet wool, and without wringing it out, place it in the large flat pan. It will be much too large to fit flat of course, so with both hands distribute the cloth over the bottom of the pan as evenly as you can. Take a few minutes to

76

Flash. Craftsman Studio design, hooked by Margaret Hooper. Simple geometric designs like this, based on the square, can easily be drawn directly on the burlap; the flower shapes in alternate squares can be drawn on the burlap with a cardboard template as a guide. Spot-dyed wools create additional interest in an otherwise simple design.

do this. Of course it will be wrinkled, and it is this wrinkling that will make the beautiful pattern when you apply the dyes. (The smaller the pan is, the longer it will take you to tuck the wool down to make it as evenly distributed as possible. Relax and take your time to do this.)

Now, with a tablespoon, spoon the main color on to the wool, in spots about the size of a medium apple, and about 2 or 3 inches apart. (You will use *about* 4 cups of it.)

Next, with a tablespoon, dribble in smaller amounts, and on the spaces between the rose spots, the second color. Let it overlap a little on the rose spots occasionally. (You will use most or all of it.)

Then, using the accent color, dribble it in even lesser amounts on approximately the same area as you put the second color. (You will use all of it.)

Now, with the back of a fork, gently push down the folds of cloth into the dye bath to thoroughly wet them, then sprinkle over it all the 1 cup of salt. Cover snugly with foil (you may have to join two pieces of foil together by folding two edges over together a couple of times), and let simmer over low heat for ½ hour or until the water is clear, being careful not to let it burn. (For such a large pan, put it over two burners.) When you remove the foil, watch out for hot steam!

Now rinse well. The "modern fabric" rinse cycle on an automatic washing machine may be used, and dry it either outdoors or with a warm or cool setting on an automatic dryer.

Here are some other color combinations, the first four being particularly suitable for backgrounds for geometric and oriental rugs.

#1 *over pale green, blue, or beige wool*

MAIN COLOR	Navy	½ teaspoon in 4 cups of boiling water (use all of it)
SECOND COLOR	Aqua Green	1½ teaspoons in 3 cups of boiling water (use all of it)
ACCENT	Terra Cotta	¼ teaspoon in 2 cups of boiling water (use half of it)

77

#2 *over gold wool*

MAIN COLOR	Gold	1 teaspoon in 5 cups of boiling water (use all of it)
SECOND COLOR	Maroon	¼ teaspoon in 3 cups of boiling water (use all of it)
(NO ACCENT COLOR)		

#3 *over beige wool*

MAIN COLOR	Maroon	1 package in 5 cups of boiling water (use all of it)
SECOND COLOR	Rose	1 package in 3 cups of boiling water (use all of it)

#4 *over pale green, pink, or blue wool*

MAIN COLOR	Bronze Green	2 teaspoons in 4 cups of boiling water (use all of it)
SECOND COLOR	Aqua	1 package in 3 cups of boiling water (use all of it)
ACCENT	Chartreuse	¼ teaspoon in 1 cup of boiling water (use all of it)

#5 *over pale blue or green wool*

MAIN COLOR	Aqualon Blue	1½ teaspoons in 4 cups of boiling water (use all of it)
SECOND COLOR	Reseda Green	1 teaspoon in 3 cups of boiling water (use all of it)
ACCENT	Gold	¼ teaspoon in 1 cup of boiling water (use all of it)

#6 *over white or pale gray wool*

MAIN COLOR	Black	¾ teaspoon	mixed together
	Dark Brown	¼ teaspoon	in 2 cups of boiling water (use all of it)
SECOND COLOR	Rust	½ teaspoon in 1 cup of boiling water (use all of it)	

(NOTE: on #6 pour about 4 cups plain water over it all before pushing wool down with back of fork)

#7 over pink wool

MAIN COLOR	Magenta	¾ teaspoon in 3 cups of boiling water (use all of it)
SECOND COLOR	Peach	½ teaspoon in 3 cups of boiling water (use all of it)
ACCENT	Green	¼ teaspoon in 1½ cups of boiling water (use all of it)

To get softer, diffused colors with any of the above formulas, decrease the amounts of dyes, and pour extra water over the wool before pushing down with the fork. To get brighter effects (such as for sharp accents in geometric or oriental designs), increase the amounts of dyes given to about double but do not add more water.

It is advisable *not* to cut all your wool up—just cut enough for your immediate use. It is easier to see the colors and how they combine in the larger piece of wool than in the cut strip. For backgrounds, of course, you may cut it all up and use it just as it comes.

Another use for spot-dyed fabrics is wall hangings! Young people especially are quick to appreciate the unusual beauty of these one-of-a-kind spot-dyed fabrics for decorating walls. Use the same method as above, but cut the wool smaller (the size you would like to have for your wall hanging) and use a smaller pan, such as the average-sized roasting pan. Hang the resulting spot-dyed fabric or choose features in the "design" that you would like to emphasize and hook them with similarly colored wools (to hook into wool flannel, use a very fine hook and narrowly cut strips).

12 Samplers

A sampler (see page 48) is an excellent way for a beginner to experiment with a variety of wools—in particular, tweeds, checks, and plaids that would otherwise be overlooked.

To make your sampler, just mark off small areas (about 1″ × 2″ or 2″ × 3″) on your burlap with a pencil, and outline them with a dark neutral-colored wool like dark gray, brown, or black. Then hook different fabrics in the small areas, stitching a sample of the fabric used next to the hooked piece.

The samplers illustrated on page 48 show how some checks, plaids, tweeds, and spot-dyed wools appear when hooked—mixtures often avoided by rug hookers. They all look different when worked in and often give a delightful texture and fluctuation that is not obtainable any other way.

All of the strips worked into the illustrated samplers are 100% wool except two (starred) which are 80% wool/ 20% nylon.

Fourth from the bottom (sampler A) is a square hooked with paisley strips from an old, torn paisley shawl. Paisley is much prized by experienced hookers, although it does have to be cut by hand (but please do not cut up a paisley shawl still in good condition, since they are frequently works of art in themselves and should be preserved), about ¼″ wide if you are hooking into closely woven burlap, and up to about ½″ to ⅝″ wide if your burlap is loosely woven. When the strip is that wide, fold it in your left hand with the wrong side folded in as you hook. Before cutting paisley, check the wrong side. You will see long threads running in one direction. Cut *with* those long threads, not across them, and the strips will hold together better. Paisleys are sometimes very dirty from long years of storage in trunk or attic. I use Woolite with tepid water to wash them, and the old fabric has always emerged clean and soft.

Second from the top (A) is a heavy dark brown tweed which was very loosely woven and needed to be cut wide (¼″ and by hand). This same heavy tweed is ideal for animals' eyes (see page 151). The individual threads, in black, brown, white, and yellow, can be used for this purpose too, hooking them in instead of a cut strip.

Black and white checks can be overdyed in Gold or Chartreuse dye, and the result is especially useful for flower centers.

On sampler B, along with checks and tweeds, are some spot-dyed wools: the two at upper left, the two at lower left, and the two at lower right.

Get into the habit of really *looking* at any fabric that is available to you for hooking, and before rejecting it, try cutting it by hand or machine and hooking a small sample. Only then will its potential become apparent to you.

13 Beginner's Project: Hex Sign

The folk art of the Pennsylvania Dutch provides a wealth of design inspirations for rug hookers. Hex signs, frequently seen on barns throughout the Pennsylvania Dutch countryside, are colorful designs and are easily adapted for the burlap mesh.

This hex sign project is excellent for beginners. The geometric shapes, easily worked on burlap, require no shading (you can use the suggested colors or colors of your own choice). Also, the design can be finished very quickly which is encouraging to a beginner in any craft.

You will need:

About 1 yard 40-inch-wide burlap
Hook, scissors, rug frame
Felt-tip marker

82

Iron-on transfer pencil
Pencil
Tracing paper
Wool strips in variety of colors

When swatches of graduated shades (such as Potpourri) are used, the different shades are given numerical values: the lightest shade is #1; medium-light, #2; medium, #3; medium-dark, #4; dark, #5; darkest, #6.

Using good-quality tracing paper from an art supply store, trace the design (fig. 23), using the iron-on transfer pencil if possible.

Place the tracing paper pencil-side down on the burlap. Using a preheated iron, rub it over the tracing paper, taking care not to let the pattern shift. Press down a minute or two to transfer the lines. If necessary, go over any weak lines with waterproof felt-tip marker. (See Chapter 5 for transferring directions.) Now you are ready to place the burlap in the frame of your choice. By using a frame, the burlap is kept taut and easy to work with, freeing the hands for the hooking process.

I show two possible ways (page 87) to hook the hex sign. The first one has simple outlining with flat colors filling the motifs. I used Potpourri swatches (available from Dorr Woolen Company);* you can use similar colors or work out your own. My colors were Talisman 6 for the heart, 5 for the large red petals, 3 for the small peach petals, and 1 for the border background next to the waves; Aqua 5 for the dark teal petals and 2 for the small blue petals; Olive Green 5 for the large green petals and Orange 3 for the small yellow petals. The background is off-white. I cut my wools ⅛" wide.

Start by outlining the heart, hooking right on the line (or just slightly *inside* the line). Then fill it in. (Beginning hookers sometimes try to pack in too many loops, so remember the rule that loops should just comfortably touch each other and not be too crowded.) Put one line of off-white (background) around the heart to preserve its shape. Next, with dark blue, hook one line on the small circle which sur-

*Guild, New Hampshire 03754. Also available from W. Cushing & Co.

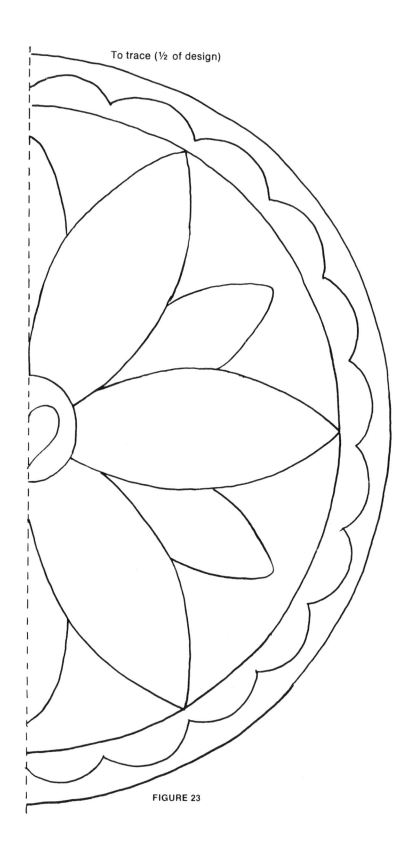

To trace (½ of design)

FIGURE 23

rounds the heart. Hook one line of off-white just inside it to preserve the circle's shape.

It is important to hook one line around any motif before hooking whatever is next to it. By doing this you strengthen and reinforce it so that its shape doesn't get distorted.

Next, fill in the remaining background around the heart and inside the circle. Try to keep your loops even in height.

Hook the large petals, first outlining them in dark blue, then putting one line (of the correct color for that petal) inside the dark blue line, before filling in the rest of the petal.

Next, outline the small petals and fill them in as above. The outer large circle is hooked next, then the inner circle, in dark blue. Then hook one line of dark blue on the line of scallops, with another line next to and inside it. Fill in remaining spaces with dark blue.

With the pale peach, hook one line inside and next to the outer blue line, then one line next to the scallop edge, then fill in remaining spaces with the pale peach.

Finally, fill in the background around the rosette, first putting one line of background next to the petals as noted before.

Now look on the back of your hooked piece. Are there any places that haven't been covered? (These are easier to see on the back.) If so, fill them in. Is the back smooth without any strips left hanging? If there are some, hook them through to the front and snip them off even with the loops.

If the back is not smooth, but lumpy, then you are not pulling your loops up properly. In the future, check the underside with the fingers of your left hand as you hook to make sure you are keeping the underside smooth and not twisting the wool strips.

The second way to hook the hex sign illustrates the use of graduated swatches, which have up to six values of one color (from light to dark). This project also uses Potpourri swatches: Wood Rose, Bronze Gold, Bronze Green, and for accent, small amounts of Aqua. Two light values of Bronze Gold are intermingled for the background.

Start in the center again, outlining the heart with Wood

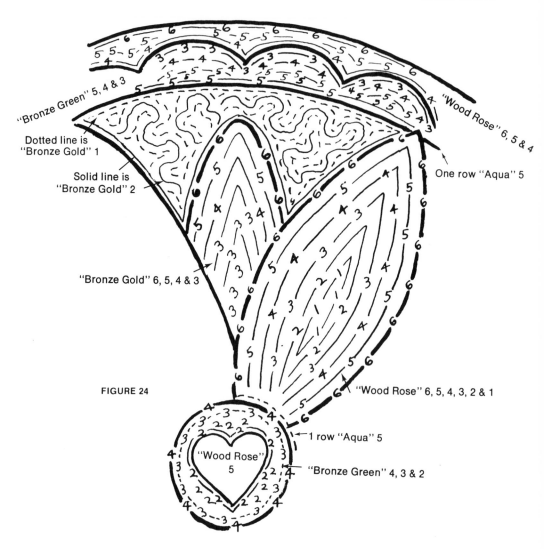

FIGURE 24

Rose 5, hooking right on the line (or just slightly *inside* the line). Then fill in the heart, being careful not to pack in too many loops. They should just comfortably touch each other. Next, hook one row of Bronze Green 2 next to the heart, then on the small circle surrounding the heart, one row of Bronze Green 4. Outside that line, hook one row next to it of Aqua 5. Now fill in the area around the heart with a row of Bronze Green 3 next to the circle; fill any remaining space with Bronze Green 2.

Hex Sign. Designed and hooked by Joan Moshimer. Two different ways to hook the same pattern are illustrated. On the left, the design is simply outlined and then filled in with flat, bright colors. On the right, several different values of one color are used in each motif to give a more three-dimensional look to the pattern.

The six large petals are all done the same, using all six values of Wood Rose. Start by hooking the dark on the outline and working your way in as shown, finishing with the lightest value in the center.

Hook the six smaller petals next, using Bronze Gold 6, 5, 4, and 3 as shown. Next on the inner circle of border, hook one row of Aqua 5; next to that, a row of Bronze Green 5. Also hook a few loops of the same in the scallops as shown. Outline the scallops with a line of Bronze Green 3. Using Bronze Green 4, fill in any remaining space in the scallops. With Wood Rose 6, hook a line on outside circle, then hook a row of Wood Rose 4 around scallops, and fill in remaining spaces using Wood Rose 5.

The background is done with the two lightest values of Bronze Gold (fig. 24). The darker one is used to outline the petals and the lighter one is hooked next to the circle. Then, using the darker one again, hook it in a random shape as shown. Finally, fill in all remaining spaces with the lighter value. Doing it this way gives an attractive mottled look.

Now as before, study the back of your hooked piece and make sure that you have not left any areas unhooked. (It is easier to see them on the back.) If you find any, fill them in. Is the back smooth, with no strips left hanging? If there are some, hook them through to the top side and snip them off even with the loops.

Don't be too concerned if this first project in hooking is not perfect—it is not supposed to be. From this you learn what to do and what not to do. In the future you will look back on it with affection as you see how much you have progressed.

14 Geometric Designs

Rug hookers refer to any design in which a motif (or motifs) is repeated several times in a formal arrangement as a geometric. A geometric can resemble the very earliest American hooked rugs or it can be innovative and very modern in appearance—it depends entirely on the way a geometric pattern is hooked and on the colors used. Cut the wool wide and use leftover wools in hit-or-miss fashion, and you have a primitive or early American rug. Or select a sophisticated one-color scheme, shades ranging from dark to light, and you have a very modern rug.

Geometric designs have been popular since the early days of rug hooking in this country. For one reason, they don't require elaborate patterns but can be drawn directly on the burlap with a sharp-pointed pencil (charcoal was originally used) using the burlap's mesh as guidelines. Or, as in Bubbles (p. 95), a dinner plate or cup is all that is needed to draw simple circular patterns directly on the burlap. Another reason for the sustained popularity of geometric designs is that leftover wools can be hooked in without further dyeing—hit-or-miss hooking—with very attractive results.

LOG CABIN

Log Cabin, one of the most interesting of all patchwork quilt designs, can be attractively adapted for a hooked rug. In traditional patchwork, the squares are half light and half dark, and the many possible relationships of the light and dark areas determine the overall pattern.

The pattern is a series of 6-inch-square blocks, with three smaller squares spaced evenly inside each block. To draw this pattern directly on to your burlap, use a pencil to make a 6″ square. Then measure ¾″ in and make a smaller square. Inside it, measure ¾″ in and make a still smaller square. Repeat once more. You now have three squares inside the 6″ square. The smallest one measures 1½″ × 1½″ (fig. 25).

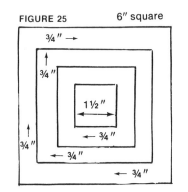

Now, by simply adding six short lines (see the dotted lines, fig. 26), the pattern emerges. Notice that the direction of the short lines alternates. Each block should contain three long L shapes and three short L shapes, in alternating positions in adjacent blocks.

Draw as many blocks as desired, then surround with a 2″ border (fig. 28). As shown in Figure 27, draw over all pencil lines with a waterproof felt-tip pen.

FIGURE 26

FIGURE 27

Draw over pencil lines with a
(waterproof) felt tip pen

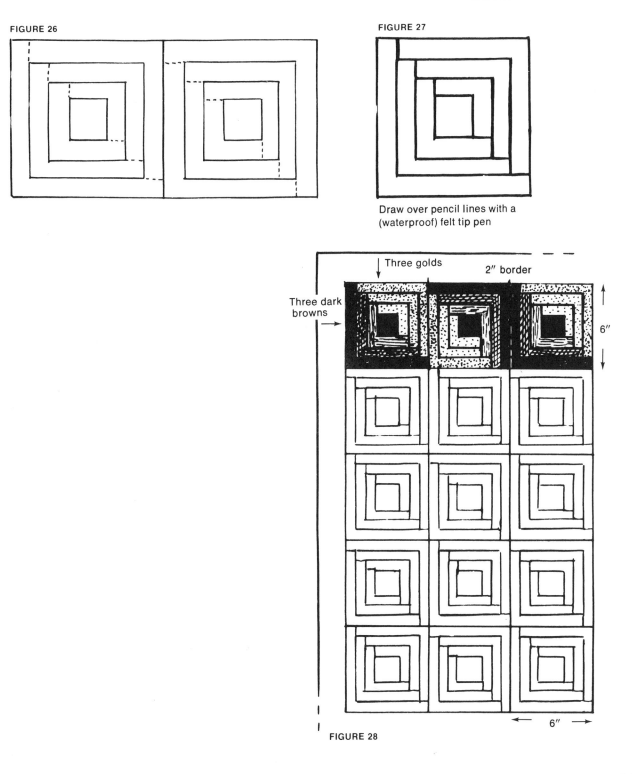

Three golds

2" border

Three dark
browns

6"

6"

FIGURE 28

There are countless ways to hook this lovely design. One very effective method of shading, popular with quiltmakers, is to shade the three longer L shapes in each block darker than the three shorter L shapes (see fig. 28); note that the position of the dark L's will alternate in adjacent blocks. Fill the small center squares with a dark color, and remember to outline all shapes with a dark contrasting color.

To follow this scheme, choose three dark values of one color—say, three browns (some plain and some tweeds, just as long as you feel they are generally dark): one *very* dark, one medium-dark, and one medium. They are to be hooked into the three long L shapes, with the darkest on the outside as shown in Figure 28. Next, choose three lighter values (of the same color or of a contrasting color). These could be in the yellow family: a gold (for the darker value), a yellow (for the medium value), and a cream (for the lightest value). These too can be mixtures or plain wools. Finally, for the center squares, use dark blue or brown or green tweeds. Whatever you choose, use it also in the border.

Do not feel that you must have enough of one color to last throughout the whole rug. Look at pictures of quilts made in this design, and notice how much substituting is done. This is the whole point of Log Cabin—it is *meant* to use up odd scraps and leftovers, and this is just what makes Log Cabin so frequently a delight to the eye.

If you want to use larger blocks than 6 inches square, just remember that the small center square measures one-fourth of the large square; the distance between each square is equal to one-eighth of the large square. Thus, for a 9″ square, the small center will measure 2¼″ × 2¼″ and the distance between squares will be 1⅛″.

WINEGLASS

Wineglass is one of the easiest design of all to draw directly on burlap. Measure off the rectangles (4″ × 5″ is a good size. Two other workable sizes are 3″ × 3¾″ and 3½″ × 4⅜″).

FIGURE 29   FIGURE 30

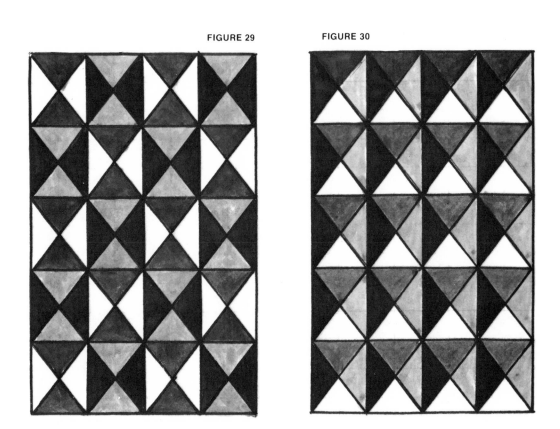

Next, draw the diagonal lines as shown, add a border—and there it is!

Figure 29 shows the pattern that emerges when alternate blocks are shaded the same. I used a color scheme in which the wineglasses in block A are dark red with a medium blue used at the sides, and in block B, the wineglasses are light red with dark, dull blue at the sides. All the outlining is done with bright blue, and the border with dark, dull blue and dark red.

In Figure 30, the results of another shading method are shown. Every rectangle is made the same with the left triangle dark green, the top triangle medium green, the right triangle medium-light yellow-green, and the bottom triangle gold. Outlining can be a dark contrasting color such as blue, rust, or brown.

Navaho. Designed by Joan Moshimer, hooked by Louise Johnson. This strong graphic design was inspired by the sturdily woven geometric rugs of the American Indian. Dark brown was used for all outlining, terracotta reds, greens, golds, and browns for the diamonds, and terracotta for the thunderbird in the center. Although these warm earth colors are typical of Indian designs, this pattern would be equally attractive hooked in a contemporary black and white scheme or even in a scheme of delicate pastel colors.

94

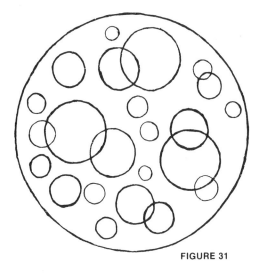

FIGURE 31

BUBBLES

Many antique rugs have patterns based on objects readily at hand. Dinner plates and cups were frequently used as templates—and still can be used effectively. Any object with a circular edge—such as a drinking glass—can be drawn around. Or to experiment first, dip the object in talcum powder and then press it down on the burlap at random. Repeat this process as many times as necessary to make an attractive design. Try different arrangements with the talcum powder, brushing away any mistakes, and when you have a pleasing arrangement, go over the lines with a felt-tip pen.

For Bubbles, intended for a chair pad or pillow, three sizes of circles can be used: a regular highball glass, a juice glass, and a bottle cap.

For the simplest circular arrangement, see the antique hooked rug on page 7—how modern the design looks!

BABY'S BLOCKS

Another design adapted from a quilt pattern has many names including Baby's Blocks, Pandora's Box, Tea Box, Illusion, and Stair Steps. This pattern is easy to draw directly on the burlap and it can be made any size. I am suggesting only a few possible ways to hook it. If you take a little time to experiment with your colored pencils and graph paper, you will discover many more.

To draw Baby's Blocks directly on the burlap, draw horizontal lines 1½″ apart using a sharp-pointed pencil, pulling the pencil between two threads in the burlap weave. Then draw vertical lines every 2¼″ (fig. 32).

Next, trace the diamond shape in Figure 33. Turn the tracing paper upside down on some lightweight cardboard

95

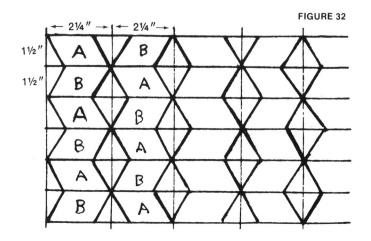

FIGURE 32

and go over the lines with a sharp-pointed pencil. Carefully cut it out. This is the template.

Place the template over horizontal and vertical lines where they cross each other, lining it up carefully. Draw around it with a waterproof felt-tip pen; also go over the horizontal lines with a felt-tip pen (except where they and the vertical lines appear inside the diamonds). Outline the design with a 2″ or 3″ border.

By filling each shape marked A (fig. 32) with dark strips and each B with light, an interesting cube pattern emerges (see fig. 34). The diamonds can be filled in with a check material or spot-dyed strips or even a graduated swatch, shading from dark at the edge to light in the center. Or they could be filled in with multicolored leftover wools.

A fresh, clear-cut scheme (fig. 35), inspired by Portuguese tiles, uses navy blues to outline the blocks and to fill in shapes numbered 2. Then in 1, use natural or bone color; in 3, brick reds; and in 4, rich old golds.

An interesting diagonal pattern emerges in Figure 36. Try making A shapes all alike, using a light value for L's and one slightly darker (of the same color) for D's. Or you might make L and D both the same to accentuate the diagonal lines.

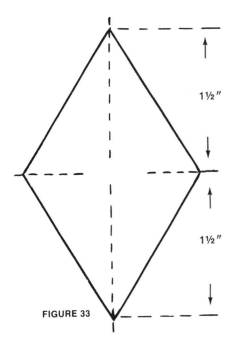

FIGURE 33

1½"

1½"

FIGURE 34

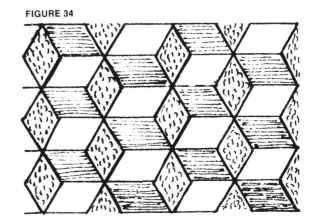

FIGURE 35

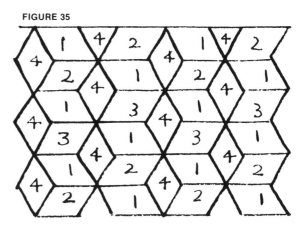

FIGURE 36

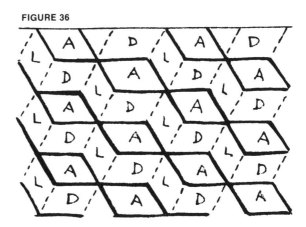

Origin unknown. This early primitive geometric was hooked on homespun linen in a simple repeat design. The pattern was probably drawn directly on the burlap with a template as a guide. The center motifs were hooked with a red tweed, outlined with greens against a black ground. Golds, browns, and whites were also used in this effective and charming design. (Private collection)

15 Intermediate Geometric Designs

The designs in this chapter are more difficult than those in the preceding chapter, but they are well worth the effort.

HOUND'S TOOTH PATTERN

A perennial favorite in suiting or coating material for both men and women is the hound's tooth pattern, a design that frequently appears in wallpapers, carpeting, and fabrics.

Hound's tooth is based on a square (see dotted lines in fig. 38). A template is needed to draw this pattern on the burlap. Make it by tracing Figure 37, then turn the tracing paper upside down on some lightweight cardboard and go over the drawing with a sharp-pointed pencil to transfer it to the cardboard. Next, carefully cut out the shape, using scissors or a single-edge razor blade. Be precise. Note: if smaller or

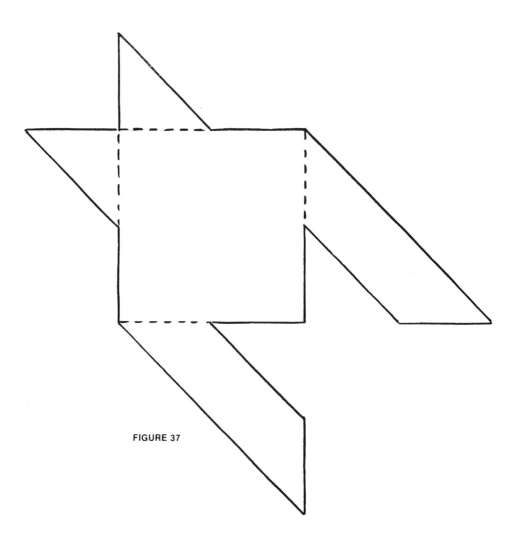

FIGURE 37

larger templates are desired, you can easily draw your own
of course, using ¼"-grid graph paper.

To set up the design, start in the upper lefthand corner of
your burlap about 6" in (or more if rug is to be large) from the
edge to allow enough room for the border. With a pencil draw
a horizontal line and vertical line (see Fig. 38, A and B).
Measure down 1" and draw another horizontal line. Measure
down 2" and draw one more horizontal line. Repeat this
second line several more times. These lines are the guidelines
for exact placement of the template.

100

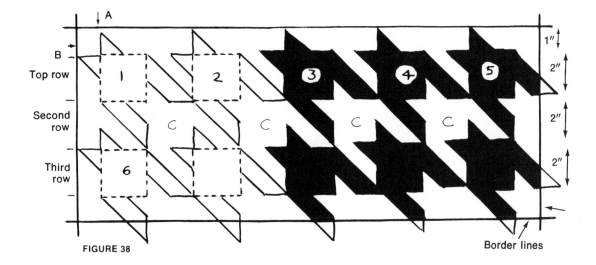

FIGURE 38

Using the upper lefthand corner as a starting point, place template as shown (fig. 38) in position marked 1 and carefully draw around it with a fine felt-tip marker. At 2, place template again and draw around it, carefully lining it up to be even with the pencilled horizontal line. Repeat as many more times in top row as needed.

An interesting thing to note is that there are squares formed *between* the squares. Now go to the position marked 6—this will become your third row—and place template as shown, drawing around it. Repeat four more times. You will now see that a second row of hound's tooth was formed by rows one and three, and these shapes are identical to the ones you have drawn. (When you hook them they should be in a contrasting color to the ones that were drawn.)

When as many of these shapes as needed are drawn in, draw a border line at the points indicated (fig. 38) to give a balanced look, then draw in a border of desired width, if a border is desired.

There are many ways to hook hound's tooth, but perhaps the most effective way is to choose two contrasting colors, as in a tweed fabric. These could be black and white, tan and brown, pale yellow and dark gold, light blue and navy—any two colors (or a light and a dark of one color) pleasing to you.

101

MONTEREY TILE

Here is a geometric design with a Spanish feel to it. The one shown on page 52 features blues, rusts, and gold, but it is easy to substitute your own favorite colors.

Figure 39 shows one quarter of the design. By tracing it and fitting together four of them you will have a completed tile which can be repeated any number of times to make any size rug.

My rug has six tiles, and its size is 23″ × 34″ (each tile measures about 9¾″).

To hook you will need:

Potpourri Bittersweet: about 6 swatches
Potpourri Blue: about 6 swatches
Potpourri Orange: about 3 swatches
Medium-dark green wool: about ¼ yard
Dark blue wool (for border): about ⅓ yard
Medium-dark blue wool (for border and background): about ½ yard
Beige wool (for background): about ½ yard

When working with graduated swatches (such as Potpourri), it's easiest to scale the shades numerically: #1 designating the lightest shade; #2, medium-light; #3, medium; #4, medium-dark; # 5, dark.

Start hooking at the center of the tile, using the Bittersweet swatch, values 5, 4, 3, 2, and 1, first outlining with 5, then filling in the middle area with 3, and finishing it with 2, 1, and 4 as shown in Figure 39.

Next, hook A using Blue 5, 4, and 3 as shown. The scroll marked B is done next, using the green wool and Blue 5, 4, and 3.

C is hooked next, using Bittersweet 5 to outline, then fill in with Orange 4, 3, and 1 as shown.

Next, hook D using a line of Orange 1 to outline, then hooking Bittersweet 5, 4, 3, 2, and 1 as shown.

The smaller motif, E, which comes between the larger ones,

is hooked next, using Bittersweet 5, 4, and 3 with Orange 3 and 1 in the center, F, as shown.

Finally, fill in background areas using beige and medium-dark blue as shown, first hooking one row of the background around the motifs to hold their shapes.

To complete your rug, hook one row of Bittersweet 4 or 5 (or whatever you have left over) all around the outside, then about three rows of green, then about seven rows medium-dark blue, and finally, about fourteen rows of dark blue. The completed border should be about 2½″ wide.

FIGURE 39

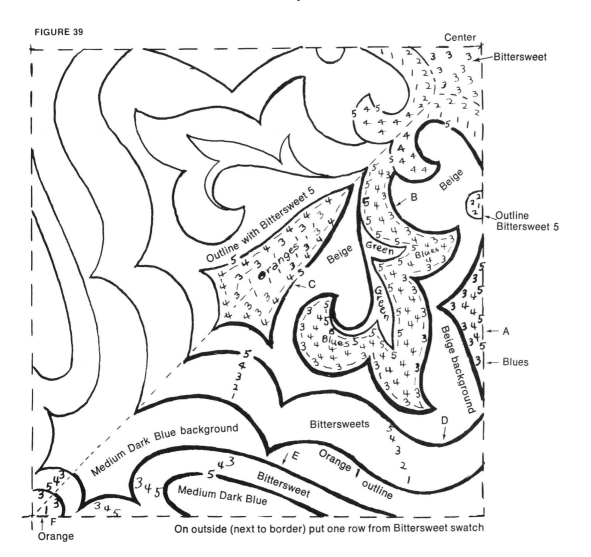

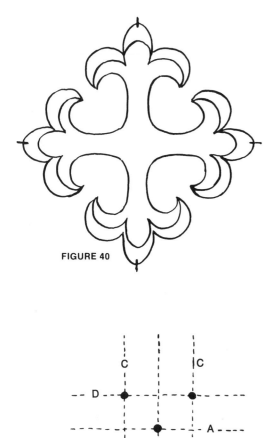

FIGURE 40

FIGURE 41

CLASSIC

Classic is a simple but stunning design. The motif can be repeated as many times as you wish to make any size rug.

With tracing paper, copy Figure 40, then turn your tracing upside down on some lightweight cardboard and go over the drawing with a sharp-pointed pencil. (This will transfer it onto the cardboard.) Next, carefully cut out the shape (an X-acto knife is good for this, or a single-edge blade). To make a pillow (see fig. 41), take a 22″-square piece of burlap and fold it twice to find the center. With a sharp-pointed pencil draw lines A and B, pulling the pencil down between two threads of the burlap. Place template exactly at center and carefully trace around it with felt pen. Next, measure off and draw lines C and D with a pencil. (These will be 3½″ from lines A and B.) Where they intercept, draw four more motifs, using your template. Now measure 6″ from exact center, and draw a 12″ square outline all around. Measure another 1½″ beyond that and draw another square which will measure 15″. This is the finished size of pillow. If you wish, draw an inner border.

To make a rug, repeat the guidelines (3½″ apart—or wider if you wish) as many times as desired, surrounding them with a border in proportion.

Fluctuating or marbleized colors make the most effective—and functional—background for a simple design like Classic (note the attractive mottled background of Fleur de Lis, page 53).

FIGURE 42

104

16 How to Hook Flowers and Leaves

FLOWERS

There is no one correct way to hook a flower, but here are a few tips to help you achieve pleasing results:

1. Keep the background color in mind at all times, especially when hooking the edges of the flower. Flowers must show up well against the background, and to do this the edges must be either lighter or darker; if they are about the same value they will blend into the background. There may be exceptions to this rule, such as when we *want* an unimportant flower to blend into the background; then the flower can be hooked in values similar to those used in the background.

2. A caution about blues and yellows: if they are too bright, they will seem to leap out of a rug—so select *soft* blues and *soft* yellows and golds. Again, you can turn this to your advantage if you want a rug that will make a "bold statement" for your floor or wall.

105

3. When selecting flower colors, please do *not* feel bound to use realistic colors for that particular flower. Choose whatever colors you want to make an attractive rug.

4. Don't overlook your local library as a rich source of information if you are in doubt about the shape of a particular flower.

5. The petals of a flower should be hooked in order of their proximity to you. Get into the habit of analyzing which petals are nearest to you or which *portions* of a petal are nearest to you, such as a "turnover" (a term used by rug hookers to describe the way petals frequently curve or twist over). The nearest is hooked first, and the farthest, last. Take time to study Figure 43; the petal marked #1 is hooked first. This rule applies too when there is a group of flowers, some overlapping others; the top flower (the one nearest you) should be hooked first.

FIGURE 43

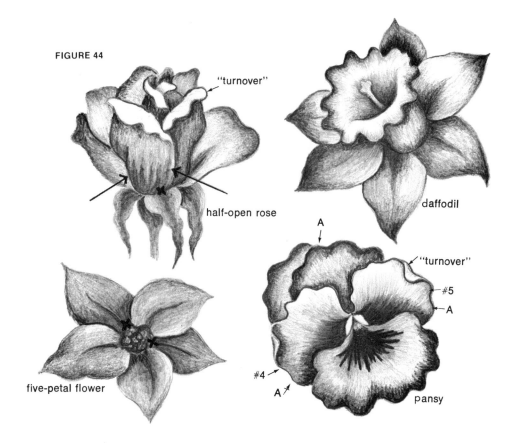

FIGURE 44

"turnover"

half-open rose

daffodil

"turnover"

A

#5

A

five-petal flower

#4

A

pansy

6. Whenever you want any part of a flower to stand out (such as a turnover), hook it with very light values, and surround it with dark and medium values (see fig. 44).

7. The beginner frequently has trouble keeping petals separated where one overlaps another. One solution is to make the edge of the top petal *lighter* than the lower petal.

Or occasionally you may want to make the edge of the top petal *darker* than the lower petal (see A, fig. 44).

8. Where the lower part of petals come together (as in rose in fig. 44), it is desirable to let the shadows blend together without much separation.

9. When hooking a rug with a central bouquet, the usual place to begin is in the center of the bouquet. This is called the focal point, the point to which the eye is naturally drawn

107

first. Usually the most important flowers are here, with the other flowers subordinate to them.

10. Hook just *on,* or slightly *inside,* the lines of a petal. Don't pack too many loops into the petal.

11. The direction in which the loops are hooked—called "directional lines" by rug hookers—is important: this gives contour to the flower. The directional lines flow from the base of the petal to the tip. In the case of a rounded petal (as in the pansy), the directional lines still start at the base, then fan out. (See examples in fig. 45.)

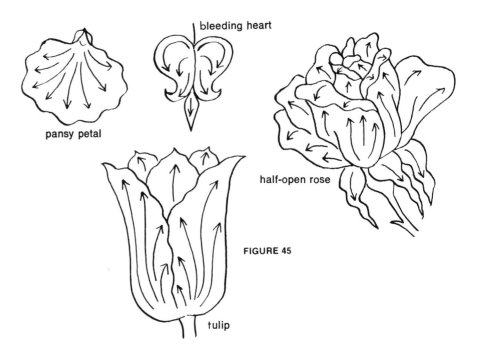

bleeding heart

pansy petal

half-open rose

FIGURE 45

tulip

12. Before hooking a petal, decide how light and how dark the petal should be. Be guided by whether the petal is near to you or further back; also, keep in mind whether the background is light or dark. If the petal is near to you, then it could be fairly light. If it is further back, it could be dark, especially if the background is light (see fig. 44). If the background is dark, then the petal must be light enough to show

108

FIGURE 46

up against the background (see fig. 46). Common sense is, of course, your best guide. After deciding just how light and how dark your petal should be, the first thing to do is to hook in the darkest part at the base of the petal. Next, hook in the lightest part, and finally, hook in the intermediate values. (Note: if you hook the darkest part, then hook in the next shade, and so on, leaving the lightest until last, chances are you will run out of space, which is the reason to get that important lightest part in early!)

13. Now is the time to talk about "fingering," the method of hooking in different values of one color so that the shades blend with one another in a natural-looking gradation from dark to light. To achieve this natural look, the different values are each hooked in sharp rises and falls that somewhat resemble fingers (fig. 47).

FIGURE FINGERING

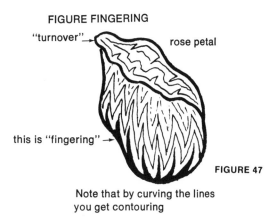

"turnover"

rose petal

this is "fingering" →

FIGURE 47

Note that by curving the lines
you get contouring

14. In Figure 44 are several flowers shaded against a light background. Notice that on the edges of the petals there are only medium or medium-dark values to insure that they will show up well against that light background. Notice too, at any point where two petals adjoin each other, they contrast with each other—the top one is usually lighter and the underneath one is usually darker. This helps to give character and form to the individual blossoms as well as to separate them. On the pansy the two middle petals (#4 and #5) have a light edge where there is a petal behind them, but a darker edge where they are against the light background.

109

To summarize, four main points need to be remembered when hooking a flower.

1. The edges must show up against the background.
2. The petals have to be hooked in the right order.
3. Hook in directional lines to give contour.
4. Shade from dark to light to give contrast and separation to the petals.

LEAVES

Leaves figure prominently in hooked rugs, either in combination with flowers or fruit or as the dominant feature. They are endlessly fascinating to hook, and while we generally think of green as the proper color for them, in nature they can be almost any color imaginable, from the familiar autumn hues of yellows, golds, oranges, browns, reds, and wines to dull gray-blues and purples, with the greens ranging all the way from chartreuse to turquoise.

Many of the tips for hooking flowers apply to leaves.

1. The choice of background is crucial. Hook a small patch of it near the leaves so that you can constantly check to make sure your leaves will show up well against it.

2. Hooking in directional lines helps to give contour (fig. 48). The veins in a leaf are excellent guides for contouring.

3. Veins are an opportunity to introduce contrasting color into leaves. Avoid a hard, flat line. Spot-dyed wool is excellent, especially if the colors are similar to the flowers near the leaves. Since only a single line is usually used for veins, even if the spot-dye is bright it is seldom "too much."

4. An easy way to hook leaves is to use green spot-dyed wools to fill in the whole leaf area. For the spot-dyed wool, use two or three green dyes, or for autumn colors, use dyes like red, orange, and gold. (See Chapter 11 for easy directions.) Just hook in the variegated strip as it comes, or be a little selective if you wish, putting lighter values on one side

FIGURE 48

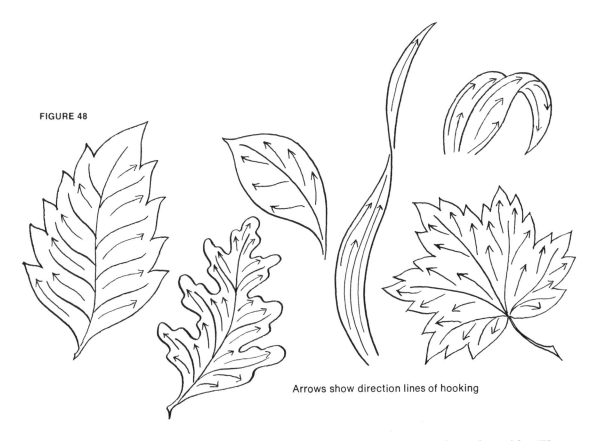

Arrows show direction lines of hooking

of the center vein and darker values on the other side. The veins can be a plain color or another spot-dyed wool in a contrasting color.

5. Study Figure 49 and notice how the shading is built up from dark to light. First the vein (in this case, spot-dyed in a contrasting color) is hooked in, then the darkest value of green (1), the medium values, (2, 3, and 4), the very lightest green (5), and finally, the background around it. (Note: if the lightest green were too light to show up well against the background we would omit it, using a slightly darker one.) Until you are experienced working with gradations, however, I suggest you work in your lightest value *before* any medium shades.

6. Don't be afraid to use your imagination. For instance, you might like to make your leaves of soft gray-blues or browns instead of conventional greens.

FIGURE 49

FIGURE 51

7. Try to get *variety* in leaves through shading. In Figure 50, you will notice some leaves are darker next to the vein, some seem to bulge because the light values are in the center areas, and others (look at the long, narrow "strap" leaf) are darker at the bottom and in the area where the leaf twists. Also, make some leaves generally dark; others, light.

8. Notice the two leaves on the right in Figure 50. They have medium and dark values at their edges which show up well against the light background. But in Figure 51, with a dark background, much lighter values are used on their edges. This is why it is important to know, from the beginning, exactly what your background color will be. As I sug-

112

FIGURE 50

FIGURE 52

gested earlier, hook little patches of background next to your leaves (never closer than ¼″), so that you *know* they are going to show up well when all of the background is finally hooked in.

9. When hooking several leaves (fig. 52), the one on top is done first, and usually in lighter tones than those underneath, especially at the point where one touches another (X). Be sure to put darker values on the one directly underneath (0). It is the contrast between the light and the dark that will separate the leaves.

If you are puzzled about how to do a leaf, do what rug teachers do. They sketch or trace the leaf and, with a regular pencil, shade in (very roughly—it doesn't have to be a work of art) the dark and medium values, leaving the paper blank

113

Trailing Rose. Origin unknown. Long red flannel underwear was most likely the main source of material for this antique hooked rug. Great skill was needed to depict the roses and buds with only one red plus black, two or three browns, and some white. Antique black is used very effectively here. (Private collection)

114

Ives Antique. Craftsman Studio design, hooked by Winona White. Hooked floral designs, always popular, require planning and skill. To be sure the flowers will show up well and not blend into the background, the background color must be decided on at the beginning and kept in mind at all times when hooking the flowers. Scrolls, used to frame the central bouquet, are usually worked in one of the predominant flower or leaf colors.

where the light values will go. This gives them an idea how the leaf will look when finished. If they are satisfied, then they (or their student) can use the sketch as a guide. Sometimes they go even further and color in the sketch with crayons or colored pencils. I think it is more important, however, to work out the *values* (lights and darks) than the exact colors.

Dead leaves strewn by the wind on a wet sidewalk, prosaic and even dismal to the unseeing eye, but what design possibilities! Pick some leaves in your own backyard—maple, grape, oak, or fig, for example—and arrange them in an unstudied, casual, pleasing way on a piece of burlap cut to the size you want your rug. Just hold them (or tape them down) and draw around their outlines. Then you're ready to hook your original, one-of-a-kind rug design.

115

17 Floral Trio Project

Floral Trio (see page 129) is a bouquet of roses and leaves that can be easily handled by beginning hookers. The finished design can be used as a pillow, picture, chair pad, stool top, or table mat.

FIGURE 53

116

To make pattern you will need:

> Burlap (approximately 20″ × 20″—the size, of course, depends on what you plan to make with finished project).
> Tracing paper, pencil, ruler, pen, iron-on pattern pencil (to enlarge, see Chapter 5).

To hook pattern you will need:

> (NOTE: If you substitute your own colors, remember these directions are planned for use with a *dark* background.)
> Hook, scissors, frame
> Small-check wool overdyed in Chartreuse dye for flower centers.
> Wool swatches. Potpourri, one of each: Taupe, White, Watermelon, Gray-green, Olive Green. Perfection swatch (available from W. Cushing & Co.): Rose Spot-dye #4.
> About ¼-yard rich brown wool flannel for background. A few strips of white wool flannel.

> CUTTING THE STRIPS: The original used ⅛″-wide strips.

Follow basic hooking directions on page 19. If you need some practice in hooking, work on the background, hooking in wavy, curving lines, not coming closer than ½″ to any part of the design. After you feel proficient at pulling up the loops, you are ready to start.

Flowers

Begin hooking at the center of the white flower, working in curving lines, and using small-check wool. When you cut up your check wool, you will notice that some strips are darker and some lighter. Use them as shown in Figure 54. The dark crescent is hooked with a finely cut strip of brown background wool.

Remember, in any wool swatch, the lightest value is referred to as 1, the next value as 2, and so on—the higher the

117

number, the darker the value. For the petals of the white rose, arrange your swatch as follows:

SWATCH		ON CHART
Taupe 5	▬▬▬	(very dark)
White 5	━━━	(dark)
White 4	≡≡≡	(medium-dark)
White 3	o o o o	(medium)
White 2	━ ━ ━ ━	(medium-light)
White 1	. . . .	(light)
White Wool	ʟ ʟ ʟ ʟ	(very light)

1. To hook a petal, work in the darkest value first; next, hook in the lightest. Thus, you have established the boundaries of darkest and lightest. Now work in the second darkest, then the next, and so on, going lighter each time until the last strips worked in are the medium-light and light values.

2. Complete one petal before going on to the next one. Hook in order. Hook petal A first (fig. 54), completing it before hooking B. Finish by hooking petal E.

FIGURE 54

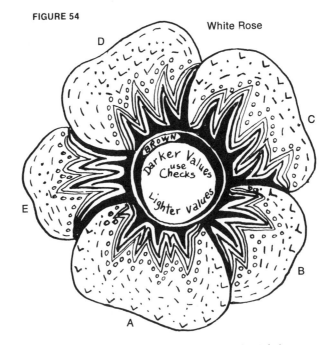

White Rose

Note: White space between center and base of petals is only to separate the two dark areas on this sketch.

118

3. There is a logical order to petals on a blossom: the one that is on top of the others is hooked first, and the one that is furthest away (underneath others) is the last one hooked.

4. A petal on top of another usually has light values on its edge; it casts a shadow directly behind it, shown by hooking a dark value on the underneath petal.

5. Although the color of your background has to be selected *first,* the actual background is hooked in *last,* after the design is completed. By visualizing how light-colored flowers would almost disappear against a light-colored background, it is easy to understand the importance of choosing your background color before you begin to hook any part of your design. By doing this you are assured that the design will be set off well by the background.

6. Although some petals are dark where they join the center, shading to light at edges (as in petals A, B, and C), others "bulge" about two-thirds out from the center. This "bulge" is indicated by hooking a few loops of light or medium-light at that spot. (This is called a highlight.) When we hook a petal like this, we usually hook medium values (or medium-dark) at the outer edge. Examples are D and E in Figure 54.

For the beige-colored rose, Figure 55, arrange your swatch as follows:

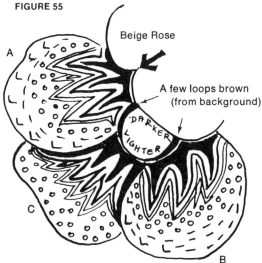

FIGURE 55

Beige Rose

A few loops brown
(from background)

SWATCH	ON CHART	
White 6	▬▬▬	(very dark)
Taupe 5	——	(dark)
Taupe 4	═══	(medium-dark)
Taupe 3	*o o o o*	(medium)
Taupe 2	- - - - -	(medium-light)
Taupe 1	ʟʟʟʟʟ	(lightest)

Follow Figure 55, making the center first as before. Then hook petals A, B, and C in order. At large arrow, be sure to hook the darkest value in a sharp "V" to help separate from the petals of the white rose previously hooked.

119

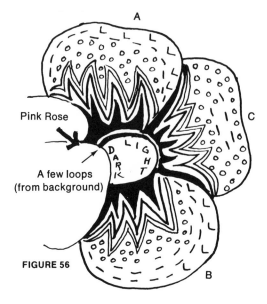

FIGURE 56

Next, hook the pink rose, Figure 56. For this, arrange your swatch as follows:

SWATCH	ON CHART	
Rose Spot-dye # 4	▬▬▬	(very dark)
Watermelon 4	———	(dark)
Watermelon 3	═══	(medium-dark)
Watermelon 2	▫ ▫ ▫ ▫	(medium)
Taupe 2	– – – –	(medium-light)
Taupe 1	ʟʟʟʟʟ	(lightest)

Follow Figure 56, first making the center, then hooking petals A, B, and C.

Leaves

Since the leaves are similar to each other, just three are charted (fig. 57). Some are hooked with just Olive Green and others are Olive Green on one side of the vein, with Gray-green on the other side. This combination of greens is very attractive in leaves. You will notice that the combination is uneven, with more of the Olive Green used.

Springtime. Designed by Anita Allen, hooked by Priscilla Lindley. This bouquet of cheerful spring flowers, framed by softly colored scrolls, illustrates the general rule that scroll borders should be kept subordinate in color to the center design, allowing the flowers to be the focal point.
Shown in color on inside front cover.

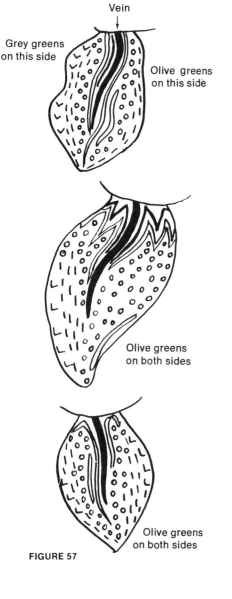

Vein

Grey greens
on this side

Olive greens
on this side

Olive greens
on both sides

Olive greens
on both sides

FIGURE 57

FIGURE 58

Since the background is dark, it is better not to use much of the dark values in these small leaves.

For leaves, arrange your swatches as follows:

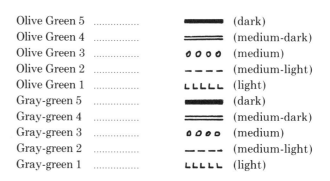

SWATCH		ON CHART	
Olive Green 5	....	▬▬▬	(dark)
Olive Green 4	....	═══	(medium-dark)
Olive Green 3	....	o o o o	(medium)
Olive Green 2	....	- - - -	(medium-light)
Olive Green 1	....	ʟʟʟʟʟ	(light)
Gray-green 5	....	▬▬▬	(dark)
Gray-green 4	....	═══	(medium-dark)
Gray-green 3	....	o o o o	(medium)
Gray-green 2	....	- - - -	(medium-light)
Gray-green 1	....	ʟʟʟʟʟ	(light)

Perfection Rose Spot-dye #4 is used for the veins. Try to select a strip that is darker at one end and lighter at the other end, so that when it is hooked in, the vein is darker at its base.

Background

Remember, in any hooking project, it is important before filling in the background to hook a line of it around all motifs (right next to them). This helps to preserve their shapes. Take care not to make the loops *higher* than the loops in the flowers and leaves. They should be the same height, or even just slightly lower, but *never* higher. When hooking the background at an area where two petals come together like this, hook *well down* into the "V." Otherwise the shape of the blossom may become fuzzy and ill-defined.

There are several ways to hook backgrounds. They can be done in curving lines or straight lines (see Chapter 4); my favorite way is to hook in randomly curving lines, then to fill in the spaces.

For other suggested beginner's projects, turn to Chapter 14, "Geometric Designs."

18 Nottingham: A Primitive Floral

Originally, primitive designs were drawn and hooked by people unschooled in art and rules of perspective, who used their rugs as a means of self-expression. (How astounded they probably would be if they could come back and see the admiration and enthusiasm generated by their works. A major exhibition of primitive hooked rugs at the Museum of American Folk Art in New York in 1974 had to be extended because of the crowds who wanted to view it.) Ruth Hall's Nottingham (see page 129) is a beautiful, modern-day example of a primitive design made with a variety of old, otherwise-worthless garments (precisely the materials the original rug hookers used). Mrs. Hall wanted to illustrate, in one small design, the basic elements that go into a floral design of the primitive type.

In spite of the rug's soft, muted appearance, there is a surprising variety of color present. Red, rose, gold, blue, brown, yellow-green, and blue-green are all there. If they

Cumberland Crewel, detail. Shading was accomplished by dip-dyed wools. Dip-dyeing over pastel-colored wools was used for the flowers, birds, and leaves. The shading of the mounds of earth was easily achieved by hooking dip-dyed wools in vertical lines.

124

Cumberland Crewel. Designed and hooked by the author (work in progress). This large rug has been planned for use in a dining room, with the design, appropriately, concentrated in the outer border; inside the border, the marbleized dark blue area is not only attractive but very practical because the fluctuating shades of blue will hide dust and soil marks.

125

FIGURE 59

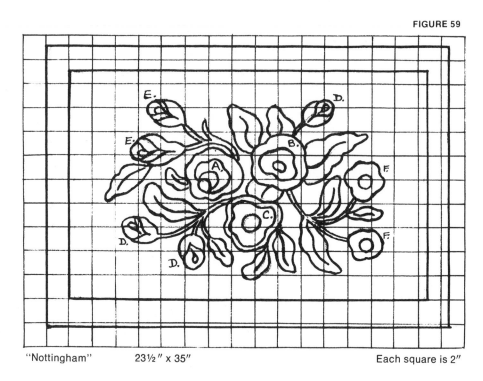

"Nottingham"   23½" x 35"   Each square is 2"

were used full strength, the result would be impossible to live with, but because they are grayed, they work together harmoniously.

Don't try to copy Nottingham exactly—just use the picture as a guide, changing and substituting to suit yourself. Then your rug will be uniquely your own.

Let us suppose that you have collected a variety of wools to use in a rug like Nottingham. They might be checks, tweeds, plaids, and plain colors, including, it is hoped, plenty of grays and browns. They should include light, medium, and dark-colored wool. If you have a large variety, you may be able to use them "as is"—that is, without overdyeing. If your colors are bright and garish, they can be toned down by overdyeing (see Chapter 10).

You will need the equivalent of about a yard and a half of light-colored tweed or plain wool for the background. If you have several that are similar, they can be combined for use in the background. (Refer to Chapters 8 and 9 for dyeing helps.)

126

For the three center roses and two rosebuds, select a couple of medium and a couple of dark tweeds to be overdyed in Old Rose. Preferably they will have a lot of gray in them, and if they have colors, Old Rose dye will successfully overdye pinks, greens, tans, light browns, mauves, light blues, and blue-greens. Dye them all in the pot together, using a medium-strength dye bath (about the same strength as tea). The object is not to obliterate their original colors, but to color them just enough to give them an unmistakable relationship to each other.

For stems and leaves, you will need more tweeds and mixtures (preferably with a lot of gray in them). Those with pink, blue, and tan in them can be overdyed in medium-strength Reseda or Dark Green (for the blue-green side of the leaves). For those tweeds and checks with yellow, gold, and green in them, try overdyeing them in Olive Green (for the yellow-green side of the leaves).

You will also need a small amount of checks and tweeds to be overdyed in Old Gold for the centers of roses and gold flowers.

For the blue flowers, you will need a small amount of gray or tan tweeds, etc., to be overdyed in weak Blue dye.

For a primitive rug like this, cut the wool wide (about ¼″) and use loosely woven burlap to make it easier to pull the wide strips through.

After organizing all your wool, the next step is to transfer your design to the burlap (see Chapter 5). Now you are ready to begin hooking!

First, hook the three center roses marked A, B, and C in Figure 60. For the center of A, use gold tweeds. Hook one line of dull brown on the heavy lines. Next, choose three or four values (dark, medium-dark, and medium) from the rose tweeds, and fill in as shown (fig. 60).

Make B like A.

Hook the center of C with gold tweeds. For the center outline, work about two rows of dull blue tweed and then outline those with blue-green tweeds. Dark is red tweed. Then select a medium-dark rose and a medium rose and fill in as shown. Outline with medium gold tweeds.

Right: Beverly Meadow. Designed by the author, hooked by Grassie Ward. A restrained color scheme was used for these large, imaginary flowers. Depending on the color used, a design such as Beverly Meadow can look very modern or very traditional. Fringe, dyed in one of the predominant colors, can add just the right finishing touch to a rug.

Opposite page, top: Golden Fruit. Designed by the author, hooked by Margaret Hooper. The wools to be used for the fruit were dyed with onion skins, which gave the colors an overall golden glow, nicely set off by the warm golden-brown background. Almost any group of swatches selected for a design can be overdyed to relate the colors.

Opposite page, bottom left: Floral trio. Designed and hooked by the author. This pattern (Chapter 17) was designed for beginning rug hookers. It can be completed quickly, yet it will give valuable lessons in shading. Illustrated on color plate G.

Bottom right: Nottingham. Designed and hooked by Ruth Hall. Nottingham (Chapter 18) is a present-day version of a primitive floral design. A variety of tweeds and checks and assorted scraps were used to achieve the mellow look of antique rugs. The same design hooked with thin strips of light, bright colors would look completely different. Illustrated on color plate G.

A

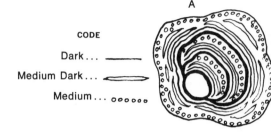

CODE

Dark... ———

Medium Dark... ◁▷

Medium... ∘∘∘∘∘∘

B   Make like A

F

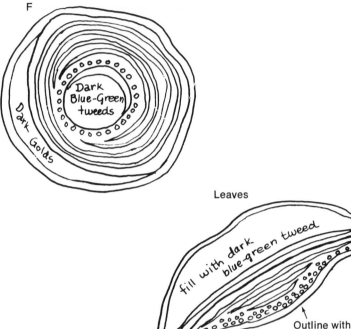

Dark Golds

Dark Blue-Green tweeds

C

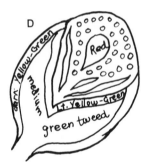

FIGURE 60

Leaves

fill with dark blue-green tweed

Outline with dark green tweeds

D

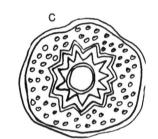

dark Yellow-Green

medium

Lt. Yellow-Green

Red

green tweed

Next, hook the three rose buds marked D, using medium-dark and medium rose values.

For the stems, use two or three rows of yellow-green tweed (not all the same—vary them).

Hook the two blue buds marked E the same as other buds, but substitute blue for the rose tweeds.

The centers of the two gold flowers marked F are outlined just halfway around as shown, using red tweed; then fill in with dark blue-green tweeds. Outline the flowers with brown tweed. Fill in with several values of gold tweed as shown.

Have fun with the leaves, using red and brown tweeds for their outlines. Then fill them in as shown, some with dark blue-greens on one side and yellow-greens on the other side.

When all flowers, leaves, stems, and buds are completed, work one row of background around them to preserve their shapes. Then fill in the background completely.

For the border, Ruth Hall's rug used colors left over from the center motifs combined with a dark check predominantly red and gray.

BORDER (background)

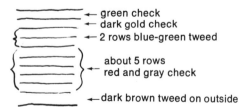

← green check
← dark gold check
← 2 rows blue-green tweed
about 5 rows
← red and gray check
←dark brown tweed on outside

130

19 Delft Daisies: Intermediate Project

The beautiful dishes made in the city of Delft, Holland, have been popular for centuries. Their graceful, simple designs, painted in varying shades of blue, are easily adapted by the rug hooker.

You might choose just one motif that is pleasing to you and enlarge it. This is what I did in Delft Daisies, with an extra flower and a few more leaves added to balance the design within the circular space.

Don't be afraid to omit or simplify anything that is too fussy for hooking. For instance, in the two large leaves below the large flower there were too many veins, so instead of six or seven, just three veins were used in my hooked piece.

To draw Delft Daisies (fig. 61), make your grid squares 1½″ for a circle 13½″ in diameter. For a larger design, 18″ in diameter, make the squares 2″. In addition to the squares, you will notice diagonal lines drawn in (see the arrow) to provide more guidelines for copying an intricate design like

Woodland Family. Designed by Anita Allen, hooked by Abby Simms. The realistic rendering of animals is one of the most difficult challenges in rug hooking. In this woodland scene, the subtle coloring of deer is skillfully captured and the standing fawn is separated visually from his mother by color—his back is hooked in light hues, the doe's body immediately behind him in dark values.
Illustrated on color plate C.

Opposite page, top: Star of the Road. Designed by the author, hooked by Bernice Bickum. This pictorial, inspired by a Currier and Ives print, has characteristically subdued coloring. Notice how important the directional lines are in a pictorial: the circular direction of hooking in the cloud of dust at the horses' hooves, for example, not only emphasizes form but also gives the impression of motion.
Illustrated on color plate B.

Opposite page, bottom: Deer in Woodland. Hooked by Hallie Hall. This charming design was adapted from a primitive rug. The handling of the deer and the setting is very different from the more naturalistic treatment in Woodland Family. Here the unusually drawn foliage provides an imaginative, fanciful backdrop. A variety of spot-dyed wools and paisley strips were used—most cut by hand.
Illustrated on color plate C.

132

FIGURE 61

1½" squares

this. If you need even more help, draw additional diagonal lines in the opposite direction.

Follow the basic helps given in Chapter 5 for drawing and transferring your design.

Remember to leave enough space between the small leaves (fig. 61, A) to allow hooking at least one row of white around them. Also, allow for one row of white to be put between the leaves and the stem (they are not attached in our version).

There is no one "correct" blue to use. The designs on the original Delft china are sometimes a dull greenish navy but more often we see a grayed purplish blue. You can dye your wool (exact formula and amounts of wool are given below) or

134

you can use either of Potpourri's blue swatches, Azure Blue or Blue, or Perfection's Blue Pansy.

I dyed more than was needed so I would have enough for future projects. If you want to dye just half the amounts of wool given, use the same amounts of dye solution (such as ¾ teaspoon for the first value, 2 teaspoons for second, etc.) but instead of using one cup of boiling water to dilute the dyes, use two cups.

Cushing's Light Blue dye is a beautiful blue, but I thought it was too bright for this project, so I chose a dye that could be considered complementary to blue to soften it without changing its "character." This would be a dye in the orange family. Mummy Brown was the one I chose because it is very orangy, although I could have used Orange, Apricot, or Rust and had similar results.

To dye your own wool, follow the basic directions (page 63), using the following formula: mix ½ teaspoon Light Blue and 1/32 teaspoon Mummy Brown in 1 cup boiling water. This is the dye solution.

Use white wool.

	DYE SOLUTION	SIZE OF WOOL
Value 1	¾ Teaspoon	9″ × 18″
Value 2	2 Teaspoons	9″ × 18″
Value 3	8 Teaspoons	18″ × 18″
Value 4	12 Teaspoons	18″ × 18″
Value 5	18 Teaspoons	13½″ × 18″
Value 6	26 Teaspoons	13½″ × 18″

I dyed more of the middle values because it was obvious that more of them would be needed for filling in the large areas in petals and leaves. This is true when hooking just about any-thing—leaves, fruit, flowers, sky, ocean, fields—we seem to need much more of the middle values as opposed to light and dark values. Keep this in mind whenever you are planning how much to dye.

For Delft Daisies I used strips cut 1/32″ wide for the blues. The white background is a combination of strips cut ⅛″ and

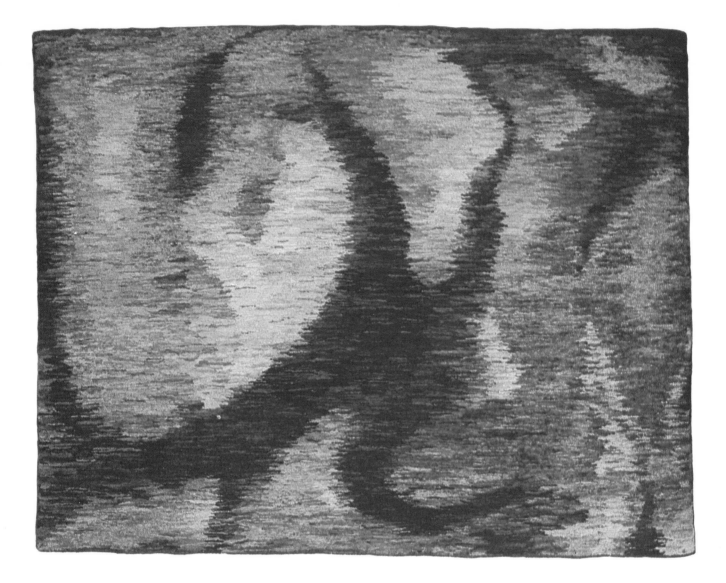

Swamp. Designed and hooked by Lydia Hicks. Abstract rugs depend heavily on color for their effectiveness. This craftsman enjoys experimenting with color and has published her formulas in dye booklets relied on by many rug hookers. She often relates a group of colors by adding small amounts of each of the dyes to the others, thus giving them a subtle harmony that is hard to define but visually stimulating. Illustrated on color plate G.

1/32″. The narrower ones were useful to work with in tight places, and since there is little difference between them, they can be combined without detriment to the finished piece.

General Hints

Use the darkest value for outlining and for the stems. In a design such as this, do not allow the background loops next to the motifs to "overpower" and partially hide the single lines of the outlining. This happens easily if you don't watch out. To avoid this, make sure that the background loops (especially next to the motifs) are not hooked higher. In other words, make them the same height or even just slightly lower than the loops of the motifs. If, when your hooking is completed, you see that some of those outlines have become partially obscured and ragged looking in spite of your careful hooking, just go back and tuck in an extra loop or two, using a narrow strip and a fine hook, then trim carefully with fine-pointed shears.

Hook the single line of the curving stems, and immediately hook a line of white on both sides of it. This insures that their graceful shape will not become distorted when the leaves and the rest of the background are hooked in.

In Figures 62-65, W represents white (also to be used for the background); 1, lightest blue; 2, medium-light blue; 3, medium-blue; 4, medium-dark blue; 5, dark blue; 6, darkest blue.

The small leaves have to be carefully hooked to preserve their shape (wide and rounded at one end, tapering off at the other end). Start at the tapered end of the leaf, hooking on, or slightly inside, the lines and working around, finishing by hooking a loop or two in the center (fig. 62). As soon as a leaf is hooked, immediately put a line of white around it, hooking close to the blue. (This preserves its lovely shape.) Then go on to hooking the next one, immediately putting the one row of background around it too. Hook all of them in this way (see page 139).

Start hooking in the center of the large flower (fig. 63). Outline the center (but not the inner circle of center) using 6.

Small leaves

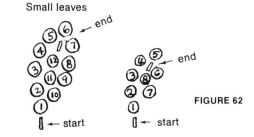

FIGURE 62

These numbers indicate sequence, not values

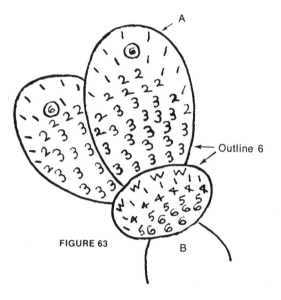

FIGURE 63

FIGURE 64

Hook center, then do the two full petals (A and B). Then hook remaining petals, completing each one before going on to the next. The three smaller flowers are all similar to each other. Their centers are similar to the large flower, but they are filled with 4 and 3. The large "brush stroke" leaves (fig. 64) are all done with 6. Hook one at a time, staying *on,* or just slightly *inside,* the line. Be careful not to pack too many loops inside them or their shape will be distorted. Hook one line of background around each leaf to preserve its shape.

The leaves (fig. 65) all have the one line of outlining (which also goes on the veins). Then 4, 3, 2, and 1 are hooked in as shown.

When all the motifs are hooked (with one line of background surrounding them), put two or three more lines around outer border line. (Note: it is a good idea to make the very outer row of hooking with extra care, making the loops slightly lower than the rest.) Then complete by filling in the rest of the background.

Now examine the back of your hooked piece for empty spaces and "tails" left hanging. If you find any, correct them before vacuuming or brushing. Then with damp press cloth, steam press thoroughly on the wrong side and again lightly on the top side.

138

Large and Medium Leaves

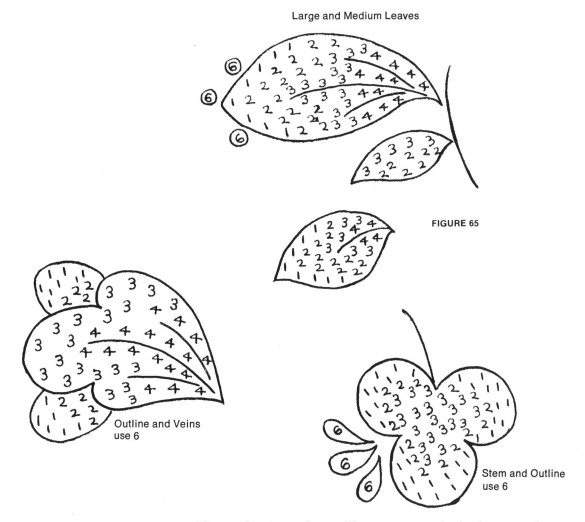

FIGURE 65

Outline and Veins
use 6

Stem and Outline
use 6

If you plan to make a pillow, you may be lucky enough to find a harmonizing blue velveteen or other fabric for the backing. If not, you could dye some more wool for the backing using the same dye formula for a medium or dark value.

139

20 How to Hook Fruit

Although we should use whatever colors please us when hooking flowers and leaves, regardless of nature, fruit, in order to be easily identifiable, should be hooked in its natural hues or at least in colors close to the natural ones. (There are exceptions—such as modern and abstract designs or adapted wallpaper or fabric designs which often require unusual fruit colors.) Swatches to be used for hooking naturalistic fruit should not be too bright.

Hooking fruit is made easier if we remember three main things: 1. highlight, 2. shadow, 3. directional lines.

In Figure 66, the small spot at "x" was drawn in to show the highlight (the part of the fruit on which the light is the strongest). After deciding where the light is coming from (arrow, fig. 66) and putting the highlight at either upper left center (as in diagram B) or upper right center (as in C), draw a "crescent moon" opposite the highlight to represent the part that is in shadow. Once the highlight and the shadow are

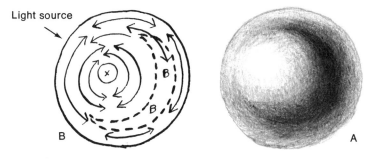

"Crescent Moon" is shown by dotted lines

FIGURE 66

decided upon and sketched on the pattern (use a waterproof felt-tip pen), the rest is easy.

After that, all that has to be done is to shade in the medium values between the "crescent moon" shadow and the highlight (using medium dark next to the shadow, then medium and medium-light values in that order).

Note that on the edges of the fruit the values are medium, which will show up well against light backgrounds. If the background is dark, then care should be taken to put slightly *lighter* values at the edges. Medium backgrounds are the most difficult to work with, and the edges of fruit must be either very light or very dark in order to show up well.

The basic rule "hook whatever is on top" (nearest to the viewer) applies to hooking fruit. Also, always hook in curving lines as in Figure 66.

If any fruit looks too flat after it is completed, make its shadows darker and its highlight lighter and watch those directional lines—they must *curve* to give the fruit rounded contours.

When space is limited we cannot use subtle gradations. It is necessary to skip some values, to exaggerate a little, in order to get from light to dark in a small area without packing in too many loops.

COLOR SCHEMES FOR FRUIT

We have many color choices when hooking grapes, apples, plums, cherries, and melons. Our choice is more restricted when hooking pears, peaches, apricots, pineapples, pumpkins, oranges, and lemons.

To plan a color scheme for the group of fruit you plan to hook, first make a rough sketch. Mark the general colors on the fruit that you don't have much color choice about anyway—for example, a peach, a pineapple, and an apricot. Since all those colors are warm colors, you should plan to have some of the other fruit in colors that are cooler, colors with blue in them, for example. So the grapes in your color scheme might be purple, and the plums (especially if they are not near the grapes) might be purplish-blues. (If the plums are near the purple grapes, you might want to make them red.) The apples could be reds and greens or, if it suits your color scheme, golden. Cherries could be red or orangy-red or even orangy.

To reiterate, start with the fruit that you don't have much color choice about and work from there, striving for balance. Balance warm colors with cool colors, light colors with dark colors.

Leaves Accompanying Fruit

Several shades of green can be selected for the leaves accompanying fruit. Blue-green, yellow-green, and an "inbetween" green are the most useful.

When most of the fruit are green (green grapes or yellow-green apples or pears), then the leaves that are close to them might look good in a contrasting blue-green. When the fruit are purple, then yellow-green leaves are attractive. Blue-green leaves are harmonious with red fruit. For variety, hook some leaves in the "inbetween" green. Avoid all greens that can be considered bright. For veins in leaves, use colors borrowed from the fruit. A spot-dyed swatch is excellent for this.

Plums

Plums can be hooked in their familiar purple hues (with smoky-blue highlights) or they can be in warm yellow-reds, greens, and yellow-greens. With such a choice of colors, they are useful (in the same way that grapes are) to help balance a color scheme.

Strawberries

Strawberries can be hooked in a variety of ways depending on their degree of ripeness. A spray of strawberries, some deep red, some light red with pink tips, and some not yet ripe in greenish-white, has great charm.

Hook a strawberry loose enough so that there is room left to tuck in the seeds later. These can be in very bright chartreuse or yellow—bright enough so that they will show up.

FIGURE 67

Pears

The first time I really studied pears I was surprised by the variety of colors they display, including yellow, gold, bronze, dull yellow-green, bronze-brown, and golden brown with "blushes" of soft orange-rose. Sometimes a half-ripe pear is greener toward the stem end and more gold-rust toward the blossom end. (See page 144.)

143

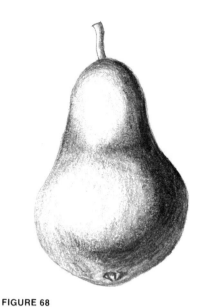

FIGURE 68

Light source

Arrows show direction lines of hooking

X Lightest areas
B Darkest areas

Apples

In many red apples, there is clear green inside the stem depression. Colors range all the way from yellow-gold to wine. The apple in Figure 69 was in reds, muted orange shades, and yellowish-green. The streaks in it emphasize the contours of the fruit, fanning out as they do from the stem depression.

Because of the stem depression, the shadow "crescent moon" on the apple extends up on the right side. There is also another shadow on the left side of the stem depression.

Apricots and Peaches

The very word "apricot" conjures up the particularly warm hue that is theirs alone. They do have tints of green and gold in their contours too. In addition to the "crescent

FIGURE 69

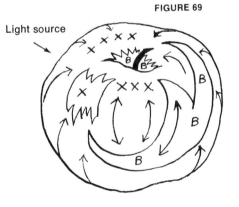

Light source

144

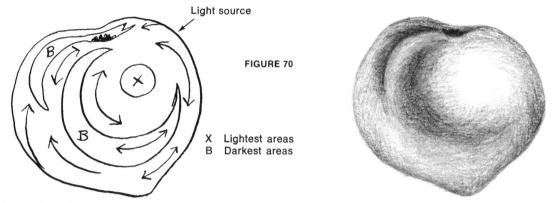

Light source

FIGURE 70

X   Lightest areas
B   Darkest areas

Arrows show direction lines of hooking

moon" shadow and highlight, there is a crease in apricots —also in peaches—that requires a shadow.

Peaches, depending on their degree of ripeness, have many hues, including gold, greenish-gold, greenish-coral, warm deep red, and "blushes" with a soft purple cast.

Cherries

Cherries can be hooked in warm reds, yellow-reds, and black-reds, as well as the more familiar rich, deep reds. They resemble apples in shape and can be done in much the same way. As with grapes, cherries are small and it is easy to pack too many loops into them. Cut the wool fine: about ⅛".

The cherry on the left in Figure 71 has the shadow crescent *away* from the outside edge (at right, where it is on top of the other cherry). On the other cherry the shadow crescent is on the outside edge (B) with another shadow (C) made by the first cherry.

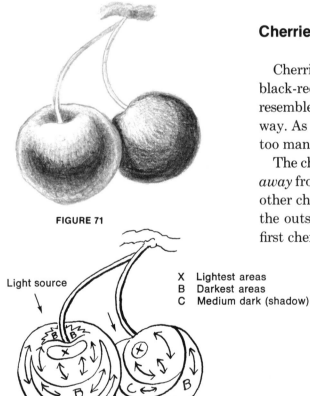

FIGURE 71

Light source

X   Lightest areas
B   Darkest areas
C   Medium dark (shadow)

Arrows show direction lines of hooking

145

Grapes

The fruit with perhaps the greatest variety of natural color is the grape, including golds, greens, brown-rose, and the whole range of purples to an almost navy blue.

The first rule to remember when starting to hook a bunch of grapes is to hook the ones on top of the bunch first. These are the ones which are complete circles, so they are easy to identify. A word of caution: it is easy to pack too many loops into these small areas causing the grapes to lose their plump roundness. The wool should be cut fine (3/32″). In Figure 72 you will notice there are five grapes numbered 1 to be hooked first, in lighter shades than the others. Those marked #2 are done next, in slightly darker values; then hook the ones marked #3 a little darker, and so on. In the remaining areas in the center (#7), fill with the darkest, dullest values, always taking care to preserve the roundness of the fruit.

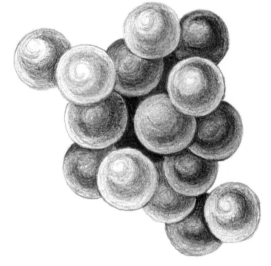

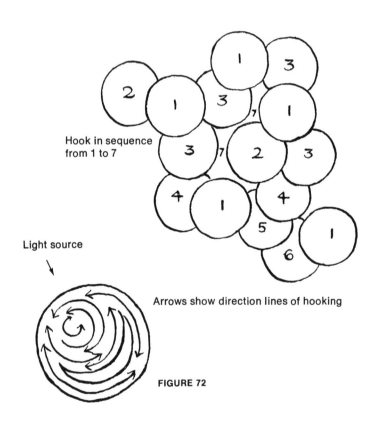

Hook in sequence from 1 to 7

Light source

Arrows show direction lines of hooking

FIGURE 72

146

Fruit. Craftsman Studio design, hooked
by Marianna Sausaman. A variety of both
warm and cool colors can be combined
attractively in pictures of fruit. In this
design, the apples are hooked with gold,
brown-orange, and dull red tones; the
strawberries, with dark reds; the
blackberries, red-purples; and the
grapes, purple. The leaves are worked in
green with light touches of brown-gold at
the edges; the cornucopia in light
browns and yellow. Note how the
directional lines of hooking, particularly
in the center apple, help to emphasize
its round form.

21 Hooking Animals and Birds

Animals and birds can be difficult to hook realistically. They should be attempted only when you have mastered the technique of hooking and have experimented with different methods of shading.

The first thing to do when hooking any animal or bird is to collect as many pictures of the subject as you can. Libraries have many large, well-illustrated books. Don't overlook children's books which can be an excellent source of color pictures too.

Also check the magazines regularly featuring nature photographs, such as *Natural Wildlife,* its edition for children, *Ranger Rick,* and perhaps the most valuable magazine for rug hookers, *National Geographic.* Any color pictures you can find of the animal you are going to hook will help you to choose the right coloring and to get the appropriate expression. If an animal's face looks right (wistful, friendly, dignified, or fierce, etc.—depending on the animal), then making the rest of him seems much easier.

Tabby Cat. Designed and hooked by Joan Moshimer. Realistically capturing an animal on burlap requires hooking expertise. Spot-dyed wools greatly simplify shading, although in this portrait of a favorite pet only commercially dyed swatches were used.

149

Eyes are the most important element in expression, and some care used in hooking them will be well worthwhile. As shown by the fifteen different eyes in Figure 73, they all vary in shape, size, and expression. Some are deep set, some protrude, some are large and lustrous, and some are small and beady. Animals and birds usually have black pupils; the irises can be brown or gold or green. When some dogs, like bassett hounds and bloodhounds, are looking upwards or sideways, some white will show in their eyes. As eyebrows on the face of a human help to give expression, so too do the lines and light and dark areas around the eyes of animals and birds.

Usually there is not much room so it is necessary to be *very sparing* in the number of loops pulled up to make eyes. It will help to pull one or two long threads from a wool strip to use in any area which is small. This is especially important when outlining eyes and any other area that needs a fine line. Pulling loops high, then cutting them with sharp-pointed shears, will also help to achieve a fine, clear line.

Begin by outlining the eye with black or darkest brown. Then make the pupil with black or off-black. Next make the iris using two or three medium values of brown (or gold or green), noting that the darkest values usually go in the top area. Then tuck in a loop or two for a highlight using white wool or a white thread pulled from a white wool strip.

Don't neglect the areas surrounding eyes. It is a mistake to just simply hook medium values up to them. Do take the time to study those color pictures you have saved. Or if you are hooking your own pet, try to decide what gives his eyes their expression. Usually it takes only a loop or two of a dark or light value tucked in to make a big difference.

If you plan to hook a picture of your own pet, observe him, make notes, and take color slides to project on a screen. Tape your burlap on the screen, project the picture on it, and trace his outline directly on the burlap with a felt-tip marker.

150

FIGURE 73

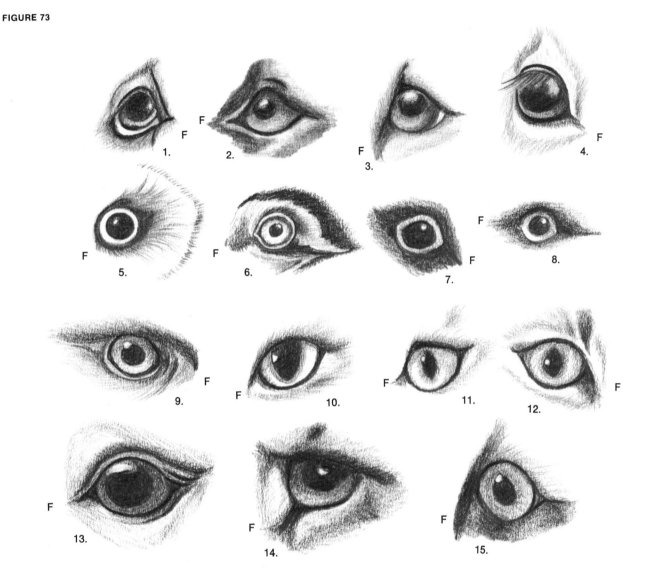

1. Right eye of a basset hound: black & browns;   2. Left eye of a labrador retriever: black & browns;   3. Left eye of a cocker spaniel: black & browns;   4. Right eye of a young deer: black & browns;   5. Left eye of an owl: black & yellow;   6. Left eye of a ringneck pheasant: black & dull gold;   7. Right eye of a Canadian goose: black & gray;   8. Left eye of a mallard duck: black & dull gold;   9. Piercing right eye of a bald eagle;   10. Left eye of a gray and white cat: black & yellow-green;   11. Left eye of a white Persian cat: black & gray;   12. Right eye of an Abyssinian cat: bronze;   13. Left eye of a horse: black & browns;   14. Left eye of a lion: black & gold;   15. Left eye of a raccoon: black & reddish brown.

152

Bluejay. Designed and hooked by Joan Moshimer. A rather loosely woven blue wool was used as the foundation material—instead of the usual burlap—for this project, and the background was left unhooked. Because pictures like this can be completed quickly, they are popular with rug hookers.

BLUEJAY PICTURE *(intermediate)*

(NOTE: Read *all* these directions first before beginning)

The first animal or bird you attempt to hook will undoubtedly be the most difficult for you. The bluejay is a good subject to start with because he is a fairly large bird with very definite coloring easy to reproduce (as opposed to the more-difficult-to-imitate subtle shading of most other birds and animals).

Trace the bird (fig. 74) and leaves on separate pieces of tracing paper; then arrange them in a design to suit yourself.

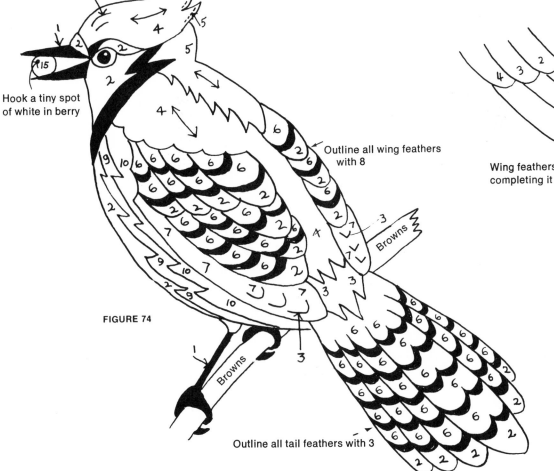

Hook a tiny spot of white in berry

Outline all wing feathers with 8

FIGURE 74

Browns

Browns

Outline all tail feathers with 3

Wing feathers. Hook 1 first, completing it before making 2, 3, etc.

153

When you have your design the way you want it, carefully lay a fresh piece of tracing paper over it and copy it for your final drawing, which you can transfer to a piece of burlap. (Note: I transferred my design to a piece of dyed wool and hooked into that instead of the usual burlap. It is easier to use burlap, however, hooking the background with a soft gray-blue *after* the bird and leaves are hooked.)

To hook the bluejay, you will need some black (#1), white (#2), light blue (#3), light purple (#4), medium purple (#5), medium blue (#6), dark blue (#7), turquoise (#8), putty (#9), beige (#10), medium-dark brown (#11), medium brown (#12), red (#15, for the berry in the bird's beak). Cut the wool very narrow, about 3/32″.

Begin by hooking the pupil of the eye with #1, being sure to hook inside the lines. Then hook a tiny spot of white in it as shown. Next, using #12, put one line around the pupil, hooking very close to it. Next, using #1, hook one line on the outside of the eye, hooking close to the brown. If you don't hook close, and if you try to pack too many loops into the eye, it will be much too large for the rest of the bird; so take a little care here.

With #2, hook the areas above and below the eye, and also at the top of the beak. Then hook the beak with #1. Also put #1 in the area between the eye and beak and on the zigzag area on neck.

Next, hook the two small lines on the head with #3. Put in a few loops of #5 as shown, then fill in the rest of the head area with #4. Hook the wings next, making one feather at a time and doing them in the sequence shown in Figure 74, putting #1 on the stripes, and #2 on the tips, but first outlining each feather with #8. (Hook the outlining slightly higher than regular hooking so that it won't get lost.)

Next, hook the bird's back, following the chart. Hook the tail feathers, making the center one first, then the side ones, completing each one before going on to the next. Then hook breast as shown, and finally, the leg (his leg should be thin —one line of hooking) and both claws.

The oak leaves (fig. 75) can be hooked with spot-dyed wool in greens (G), burnt oranges (O), and browns (B), as well as

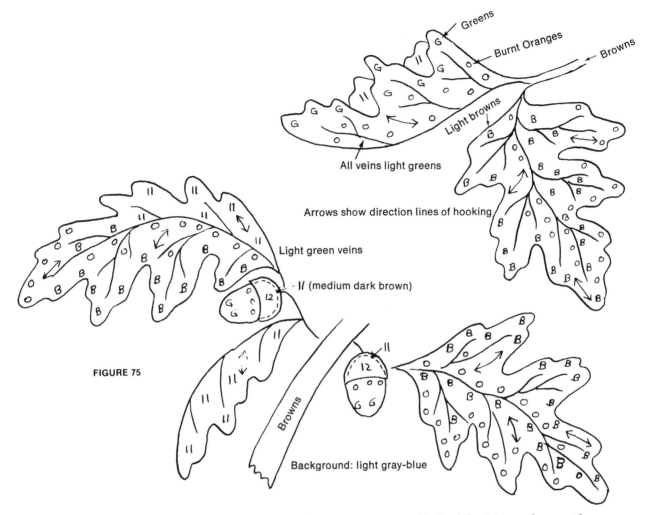

Greens

Burnt Oranges

Browns

All veins light greens

Arrows show direction lines of hooking

Light browns

Light green veins

- ll (medium dark brown)

FIGURE 75

Browns

Background: light gray-blue

#11. The acorn caps use #12 with #11 as shown, then green and burnt-orange. Hook browns on stems.

When all hooking is completed, study your bird, checking to see if the eye is bright and the beak is straight and pointed. He should have a general air of perkiness.

When you are satisfied, hook one line of the background around all motifs before filling in the rest of the background. If you decide to leave the background unhooked, make the loops at edges of all motifs quite low; be extra careful not to pack too many loops into the bird and leaves.

When completed, steam press thoroughly on the wrong side, then again lightly on the right side.

155

22 Pictorials

The next time you are out riding in the country, stop and really *look* around you. Take a long, careful look at an old barn or house. There is no harsh, flat expanse of color; the shades blend and flow. The same is true of any tree, field, mountain, or sky. Note the many greens in a country scene: yellow-greens, rusty greens, brown-greens, bright spring greens, dull forest greens, blue-greens—the list goes on in almost endless variety. Look for the deepest blue you can see in the sky. Study it a minute and you will notice it really isn't a bright or dark blue at all. Keep this in mind the next time you hook a sky because a common mistake is to make the blue too bright.

Before beginning to hook a pictorial, take a little time to study it. Decide from which side the sun is shining (even in a cloudy winter scene). This decision will determine the parts of your scene which should be highlighted and where the shadows should fall.

Old New England Coach Line. Origin unknown. Early pictorials were hooked with the freedom and gaiety of true folk art. As this typical antique pictorial illustrates, rules of perspective were not a concern—or hindrance—to the early rug hooker.
(Courtesy Shelburne Museum, Inc., Shelburne, Vermont)

Next, analyze the picture and decide what is closest to you. This is usually the most important element, the focal point, and it should be hooked first. Other things in the foreground are hooked next (such as rocks, fences, a bridge, a tree). Whatever is behind them is hooked next. Continue to work your way back, hooking distant trees, hills, and finally, the sky.

For example, look at Star of the Road, page 133. The first thing to hook in this picture would be the lady in her carriage, then the closer horse, then the horse partially hidden, and then the carriage itself. These make up the focal point.

Study the rest of the picture. Those tall trees behind the lady would be hooked before the house is hooked because they are in front of it, and the dark green bush in left foreground would be worked before the road and grass.

The bank at right could be done any time after the horse and carriage are worked, but the fence at the top would have to be done *after* the tree on the right and the dark bush, but *before* the trees that are further back.

The sky would be hooked last. Note its quiet color, depicting a dull, overcast day.

It is crucial to follow this rule of hooking first whatever is nearest to you, the viewer—it helps to preserve the shapes of objects as well as to maintain their relative importance.

The directional lines of hooking are particularly important too. Put simply, if an object is round, then the direction of the lines should be curving. A straight road would look best hooked in straight lines; a waterfall or a tree trunk hooked vertically.

In Star of the Road there are some good examples of directional hooking. Clouds of dust kicked up by the pounding hooves swirl in a circular pattern; the clapboards on the left side of the house run horizontally; the drooping branches of the weeping willow tree fall vertically—all these show clearly that the direction of the hooking helps to show shape and form.

PICTORIAL SPOT-DYEING *(casserole dyeing)*

The following formulas will help you to achieve the soft, blended colors needed for pictorials. The formulas are wonderful for leaves, ocean water, trees, fields, rocks, snow, etc. This is almost the same method as the spot-dyeing in Chapter 9, but with a few differences.

1. Cut your wool the *same* size as the bottom of a shallow refrigerator pan.
2. Soak wool in detergent as before.
3. Lay one piece of dripping wet wool in the bottom of dye pan. *Do not put on heat yet.*
4. Instead of putting your dye on the wool in "blobs" as described in Chapter 11, put it on as follows (fig. 76).

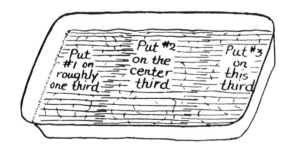

FIGURE 76

Spoon #1 on the left ⅓ area of the wool, then #2 on the middle area of the wool, letting the dyes overlap a little, then

#3 on the right area of the wool, again overlapping a little. Now, where the dyes overlap, move the back of the spoon down in a zig-zag motion to blend the dyes together. This will produce delightful inbetween blends. Sprinkle about 2 tablespoons plain salt over the wool.

Then place another piece of wet wool on top of the first, and repeat the dye and salt application exactly. Then another piece and another, putting dyes on each piece, building up to about 6 or 8 pieces, if you wish.

Now cover tightly with foil (no need to add any more water), and place in 325° oven for one hour. Remember, after removing wool from the oven, rinse well before drying.

You can achieve dark, medium, and light effects by using gray wool for the first pieces, then pastel wool, and finally white pieces. Also, if you dilute your dyes with more water for the white pieces, the results will be lighter and weaker. Don't feel that you must use all the formulas; you won't usually, unless you are doing large amounts. I think 6 or 8 pieces the size of your shallow pan (about 9″ × 12″ or 10″ × 14″) is enough to do at one time.

Some dyes are dark and look alike when you put them on the wool, but you will be pleasantly surprised when you see the result.

AUTUMN FOLIAGE #1 *(good for oak leaves)*

Dye #1: ¼ teaspoon Wine in 1½ cups boiling water
Dye #2: ¼ teaspoon Salmon in 1½ cups boiling water
Dye #3: ⅛ teaspoon Light Brown in 1½ cups boiling water

AUTUMN FOLIAGE #2

Dye #1: ¼ teaspoon Golden Brown in 1 cup boiling water
Dye #2: ¼ teaspoon Chartreuse in 1 cup boiling water
Dye #3: ¼ teaspoon Scarlet in 1 cup boiling water

AUTUMN FOLIAGE #3

Dye #1: ¼ teaspoon Dark Brown in 1½ cups boiling water
Dye #2: ⅛ teaspoon Aqualon Wine in 1½ cups boiling water
Dye #3: ¼ teaspoon Apricot in 1½ cups boiling water

SPRING FOLIAGE

Dye #1: ⅛ teaspoon Bronze Green in 1½ cups boiling water
Dye #2: ¼ teaspoon Chartreuse in 1½ cups boiling water
Dye #3: ¼ teaspoon Khaki Drab in 1½ cups boiling water
Dye over white wool and light green or yellow wool.

SUMMER FOLIAGE

Dye #1: ¼ teaspoon Green in 1 cup boiling water
Dye #2: ⅛ teaspoon Olive Green in 1 cup boiling water
Dye #3: ⅛ teaspoon Ocean Green in 1 cup boiling water
Dye over white wool and light green, pink, or blue wool.

DISTANT TREES *(grayed tones)*

Dye #1: ¼ teaspoon Reseda Green *and*
      ¼ teaspoon Silver Gray in 1 cup boiling water
Dye #2: ¼ teaspoon Bronze Green *and*
      ¼ teaspoon Silver Gray in 1 cup boiling water
Dye #3: ¼ teaspoon Khaki Drab *and*
      ¼ teaspoon Silver Gray in 1 cup boiling water
Dye over white wool and pale pink, pale lavender, or pale blue wool.

AUTUMN FIELDS

Dye #1: ¼ teaspoon Champagne in 1 cup boiling water
Dye #2: ¼ teaspoon Khaki in 1 cup boiling water
Dye #3: ⅛ teaspoon Lemon in 1 cup boiling water
Dye over medium and light greens and (for shadows) various grays.

SUNSET OR SUNRISE SKY

Dye #1: ⅛ teaspoon Coral in 1 cup boiling water
Dye #2: ⅛ teaspoon Maize in 1 cup boiling water
Dye #3: ⅛ teaspoon Nile in 1 cup boiling water
Dye over white and peach and pale blue wools.

SNOW SHADOWS

Dye #1: 1/16 teaspoon Black in 1½ cups boiling water
Dye #2: ⅛ teaspoon Ecru in 1½ cups boiling water
Dye #3: ⅛ teaspoon Aqua in 1½ cups boiling water
Dye over pale blues and white wools.

EVERGREEN TREES

Dye #1: ⅛ teaspoon Black in ¾ cup boiling water
Dye #2: ⅛ teaspoon Dark Green in ¾ cup boiling water
Dye #3: ¼ teaspoon Myrtle Green in ¾ cup boiling water
Dye over green, pink, and white wool.

OCEAN WATER

Dye #1: ⅛ teaspoon Navy Blue in 1½ cups boiling water
Dye #2: ⅛ teaspoon Aqualon Blue in 1½ cups boiling water
Dye #3: ¼ teaspoon Ocean Green in 1½ cups boiling water
This formula is fairly bright, but use some peach or beige wool (as well as gray and white) and you will get some quieter colors.

QUIET LAKE WATER

Dye #1: ⅛ teaspoon Turquoise Blue in 1 cup boiling water
Dye #2: ⅛ teaspoon Silver Gray in 1 cup boiling water
Dye #3: ⅛ teaspoon Old Ivory in 1 cup boiling water
Dye over pale gray (if you are lucky enough to have some) and white wool.

STORMY OCEAN WATER

Dye #1: ⅛ teaspoon Dark Gray in 1 cup boiling water
Dye #2: ¼ teaspoon Turquoise Blue in 1 cup boiling water
Dye #3: ¼ teaspoon Nile in 1 cup boiling water
Dye #4: ¼ teaspoon Tan in 1 cup boiling water
Dye over white or any pastel wool.

NOTE: For this one, spoon Dye #1 over the whole piece of wool, then apply the next 3 dyes as in the others, *or* omit the Dark Gray and dye over gray wool.

STORMY SKY

Same as the one listed above, but dilute in 4 cups boiling water, then proceed as directed.

It is better *not* to cut your spot-dyed wools until you are ready to use them because it is much easier to see the colors and how they combine in the larger piece of wool than in the cut strip. So cut your strips only as you need them.

23 Abstract Designs

You can be as adventurous and original as you like when creating your own rug design. Remember, hooking is an art form and you should use it to express yourself freely. For some rug hookers, abstract designs are the most enjoyable to plan and to hook. With abstract designs, there is no striving to reproduce realistically scenes or animals or flowers—your imagination is your best guide.

A talented rug hooker, Lydia Hicks, of Syracuse, New York, designed a very effective abstract rug (page 136) she calls Swamp. Here is her own description of the creation of Swamp and some excellent hints on transferring designs to burlap.

"While developing this rug I had no thought of a swamp. I just enjoyed working the curving lines and spaces. The central dark blue design is the focal point and is a little off-center. I finally got what pleased me.

"I find it takes a lot of thinking, planning, and patience to create an original design. It is also thrilling and satisfying.

The design just grows in your mind and then under your hand. What satisfaction to know that there is not another one like it in the whole wide world!

"Here are my designing and transferring tips:

"Enlarge your small drawings [as explained on page 29]. Place white nylon net over your enlarged drawing and trace the design onto the white net with a colored felt-tip pen.

"Next step. Pin or tape the net over your burlap and using a waterproof black felt-tip pen this time, draw once more over the lines. The ink should penetrate through the net and make a faint line on the burlap. All the lines can be gone over again with the marker to make clear lines.

"For colors I chose blues, greens, orange, tans, and browns. I dyed my own wool using formulas from my dye booklets, 'Triple Over-dye Book One' and 'Book Two' (available from Craftsman Studio). Occasionally I also used light and dark gray tweeds as I found them.

"I decided to do all the hooking horizontally, starting with the main design of different dark blues (some were almost black). I made all the edges of design motifs very irregular so that I could 'finger in' the adjoining colors.

"I would say to anyone making a similar design, the most important thing is to let yourself go. Be creative and *have fun.*"

Don't overlook local museums and art books as inspiring sources of abstract designs.

24 Some Final Tips and Reminders

1. Keep a scrapbook of possible reference materials: pieces of drapery, wallpaper samples, flower pictures from greeting cards and seed catalogs, scenes and delightful illustrations from children's books.

2. Collect old wool garments given by friends and family or bought at rummage sales, Goodwill, and the Salvation Army stores. Rip them apart and wash in the machine, even if they appear clean. This will discourage moths and help to make the wool soft and fluffy. These used wools can often be used "as is." Or they can be "color removed" or overdyed.

3. When planning a rug, try to decide where it will go in your home. This will guide you as to size and coloring. When choosing your colors, decide first whether it should have a light or dark background, and then what *color* background it can have.

4. Generally speaking, it is best to save your brightest colors for small areas and your softest colors for large areas. How-

ever, a common mistake is to use colors too soft and too delicate. Carpet manufacturers advise their customers to choose colors a *little* brighter than what they need, to allow for the softening of time and use. This is good advice for rug hookers too. Remember, these are rugs *for the floor* and our floors receive harder wear than any other area in our homes. So my advice is to use *slightly* stronger and brighter colors than you would normally choose—you will be glad you did after a year or two of wear.

5. To estimate how much background wool is needed for a design, allow ½ pound of wool for a square foot. Do not deduct for the design, then you will be allowing yourself plenty to work with. Another method is to cover the background area with four or five layers of cloth (four if you hook low and five if you hook high). The resulting amount is approximately what you will need.

6. When buying mill-ends, many times the strips are sewn together. It is possible to pull out this complicated-looking stitching if you go at it the right way (see fig. 78). Quite often the thread is of good quality, and it can be dyed (wind it around a dowel) along with your backgrounds and used to hem back the rug tape.

7. White vinegar, used as a mordant (mordants are used to "fix" the dye to the wool), will sharpen and brighten the color slightly, while uniodized salt tends to soften and gray the color slightly. Both are equally good.

8. When dyeing a sequence for flowers or leaves, dye extra wool in the middle shades because usually the middle shades are the ones we run out of first; proportionately more of them are used than the light or dark shades.

9. If you have made a dyeing "mistake," the wool need not be wasted, because you can always overdye it for something else.

10. Do you have some cut wool that you would like to overdye? It can be done if you first carefully lay the strips flat inside an old nylon stocking, tying the stocking in two loose knots, one above and one below the strips. Then dye, rinse, and dry as you would any other wool.

11. Keep notes on your dyeing. Buy little pin-on tags and

not like this

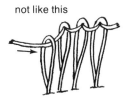

Free thread from this loop

FIGURE 78

but like this

pull →

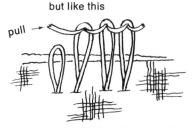

Now the thread will pull out easily

attach to a sample of each dyeing job, telling what color it was originally and what dye was used. Or glue the samples in a notebook and write the information next to each one. How these will help you when planning future rugs! It is surprising how easy it is to forget what we did last week or last month, but with your notes, all your past work will always be at your side to help you.

Leftover dyes can be stored safely in small jars. Buy some gum labels so that you can label each jar with the dye name. This is *essential*—you cannot identify dyes just by looking at them. If the dyes should "clabber," just bring them to a boil again before using.

12. Be sure to work your initials somewhere in your rug. Don't make them prominent—in fact, the viewer should have to hunt to find them. Perhaps in the background, hooked in a slightly darker shade than the background color. You can also work in the year; your descendants will be grateful. Or you may embroider initials and date on the binding tape.

13. No matter how careful we are with our precious rugs, when they are in use on the floor, an annual cleaning with one of the leading rug shampoos is good for them. Occasionally there is a stubborn stain that refuses to budge. For that reason I urge you to save some of your leftover wools from each rug—especially background wool. Put them in a little plastic bag, seal, and label. Then it is a simple matter to pull out the offending stain and hook in fresh loops. You will find it easier to pull the strip out if you pull with tweezers from the under side. To first mark the place, put a toothpick carefully through the rug from the top side.

14. When rolling up a rug to store it or to transport it, always roll it *right side out,* then you will not be putting unnecessary strain on the burlap. Wrapping your rug in an old sheet will keep it clean.

Pauline E. Gordon

JOAN MOSHIMER. The New Zealand-born
author, who studied art at the Elam School of
Art in Auckland, came to the United States
after World War II and became an adopted New
Englander. With her husband, Bob, she is
owner of the Craftsman Studio in Kennebunkport, Maine, and of Cushing "Perfection" Dyes,
a distinguished old firm which sold dyes to
many nineteenth-century rug hookers. Former
editor of *Rug Hooker News and Views* magazine, widely known as a lecturer and teacher of
hooking, she has played an important role in
the revival of the craft. She is currently on the
editorial board of *Rug Hooking* magazine.

746.7
Moshimer, Joan
The Complete book of
Rug Hooking

DISCARD
Norman Williams Public Library
Woodstock, VT